British
Buses
since
1945

British Buses since 1945

Stephen C. Morris

Publishing

Contents

First published 1995

ISBN 0 7110 2280 1

Published by Ian Allan Publishing

an imprint of Ian Allan Ltd, Terminal House, Station Approach, Shepperton, Surrey TW17 8AS.
Printed by Ian Allan Printing Ltd, Coombelands House, Coombelands Lane, Addlestone, Weybridge, Surrey KT15 1HY.

Front cover:
A Leyland Atlantean with Northern Counties bodywork, originally Greater Manchester No 7567 then sold to East Midlands, is seen at Hornchurch in 1988.
Kevin Lane

Half-title:
The one-off SMT lightweight integral bus, based on Albion running units, seen at St Andrew Square, Edinburgh.
John Aldridge

Title page:
Foden's last sortie into the bus market, in conjunction with Northern Counties, proved short-lived. Only seven were completed, two for Greater Manchester Transport. The Foden-NC had a rear transverse Gardner 6LXB engine and Allison transmission.
Ferodo Ltd

Back cover top:
A Thames Valley Bristol LL6B.
Peter Durham

Back cover bottom:
A Capital Citybus Optare MetroRider being run in before London service in 1992.
T. K. Brookes

ACE/Ward	14
AEC	15
Ailsa	25
Albion	26
Alexander	30
Atkinson	31
Austin	32
BMMO	34
Beadle	40
Bedford	41
Bristol	44
Commer	50
Crossley	53
CVE/Omnicoach	55
Daimler	56
Dennis	60
Dodge/Renault	69
Douglas	70
Duple	71
Foden	72
Ford/Thames	75
Freight Rover/LDV	79
Guy	80
Harrington	84
Jensen	85
Karrier	86
Leyland	86
Maudslay	103
Metro Cammell Weymann	104
Morris-Commercial	109
Moulton	110
Northern General Transport	110
Optare	111
Quest 80	112
Rowe	114
Rutland	115
SMT	115
Saunders-Roe	115
Seddon	115
Sentinel	120
Shelvoke & Drewry	123
Talbot	123
Thornycroft	125
Tilling Stevens	125
Trojan	125
Volvo	125

Acknowledgements

Thanks are due particularly to John Aldridge, author of the companion volume, *British Buses before 1945*, who has been particularly helpful and supportive in supplying information, has taken the trouble to read through the manuscript and even added one or two bits himself, Kevin Lane, who undertook some of the picture research, Mike Sutcliffe, who gave Kevin Lane access to his photo collection, and Mike Fenton whose work on Quest 80 was very useful. Thanks are also due to Heather, my wife, and David, my son, who have put up with a house full of reference material (having to disguise it from time to time so as not to put off prospective buyers of our house, which we were trying — unsuccessfully — to sell at the same time!) and for having to put up with a husband/father respectively who was even more irritable than usual during the production of this book.

Also acknowledged gratefully is reference to a number of publications, especially some of the PSV Circle chassis lists, a number of Venture Publishing and TPC titles such as 'The British Bus Story' volumes for the 1950s, 1960s and 1970s, the 'Best of British Buses' series, especially the postwar Daimler volume, and Doug Jack's *Beyond Reality*, plus Ian Allan publications down the years on various chassis manufacturers, such as Geoffrey Hilditch's *Looking at Buses*, Robin Hannay's *Dennis Buses in Camera*, Jasper Pettie's *Guy Buses in Camera*, and Stewart Brown's Albion and Crossley book in the same series. R. C. Anderson's *History of Midland Red*, published by David & Charles was helpful for the BMMO section, while much information was gleaned from *Buses Illustrated*, *Buses* (which I humbly recommend!), *Classic Bus and Passenger Transport* plus Ian Allan's 'British Bus Fleets' series of the 1950s and 1960s.

Introduction

Given that in 1995 there are but two British-owned bus manufacturers active in the UK market, it is remarkable that a book like this can list no fewer than 46 British manufacturers which have been active in the UK market over the last 50 years. And that is to overlook ERF, a British manufacturer which still builds buses, though not for use in this country. Some of the manufacturers listed may only have built buses in penny numbers — one or two indeed built only one each — but others were sizeable in their day. Together they represent a kaleidoscope, and an apt reminder of why those of us over, shall we say, a 'certain age', find buses so fascinating.

The following chapters look at bus manufacturers which have actively built buses in Britain since the war, not ones which have simply imported them into this country. Thus the likes of Scania and DAF, both active in the UK market, do not appear, though Volvo does with its UK-built products. It is a shame though that the list of contents reads largely as a historical catalogue, and many once familiar names are no longer with us.

STEPHEN C. MORRIS B Mus, MCIT
Shepperton, Middlesex, January 1995

British Buses since 1945

The postwar period has turned out to be a traumatic one for the British motor industry as a whole, and this is especially true of the bus and coach industry. Immediately after the war, and indeed for the ensuing 20 years or more, imported vehicles were the exception rather than the norm, and were unheard of in the bus and coach sector. Who would have thought that by the mid-1990s Britain's biggest car exporter would be a Japanese company called Nissan, that our motorcycle industry would be down to the odd niche manufacturer, and that not only would Dennis be the leading UK bus builder but that almost everybody else who was anybody was now part of Volvo. Except Bedford which had ceased to exist!

Contrast that with the situation immediately after the war when Britain could boast nine what may be called 'mainstream' bus chassis builders (AEC, Albion, Bedford, Bristol, Crossley, Daimler, Dennis, Guy and Leyland), plus other commercial vehicle builders like Atkinson, Austin, Commer, Foden, Ford and Seddon which were to come into the market subsequently, those like Maudslay and Tilling-Stevens which had been more significant before the war and would play some part, albeit minor, after the war, and the Birmingham & Midland Motor Omnibus Co, Britain's biggest company bus operator which ploughed its own furrow, building its own buses whose plain styling disguised cutting-edge technology under the skin.

The British postwar bus was a solid, no-nonsense affair. Before the war the British bus had reached a peak of refinement, and there were various interesting technical developments going on. AEC had built its first RT-class buses for London in 1939, bringing together numerous new features such as air brakes and air-operated preselective transmission packaged together in a body style which set new standards for grace and elegance and featured a very low bonnet line for improved driver visibility.

The RT was of largely conventional layout, but tentative experiments had been carried out to get the engine out of the way on single-deckers; Leyland had explored both rear engines and mid underfloor engines before the war and other manufacturers, notably AEC, were going the same way.

The war put paid to such fripperies; basic, solid, low-cost engineering was the order of the day, and only Bedford, Guy, Daimler and Bristol had been permitted to build new buses. Everyone else was concentrating on the war machine. They came back into the field from 1945/46 but generally models such as Leyland's Titan PD1 and AEC's Regent (and their single-deck equivalents, in this case Tiger and Regal respectively) cut little new ground. Nor could they be expected to; after the war it was just a matter of concentrating on getting new buses into production, simple, reliable ones at that, and never mind the frills.

It is perhaps surprising then that by the end of the 1940s most manufacturers had new ranges on the market. To the passenger most may have looked or seemed little different from what went before, but there were new levels of refinement and particularly performance, while innovations continued under the surface, such as synchromesh gearboxes to make life easier for the driver. Development that had been interrupted by the war was back in full swing.

Above:
A superb shot in the 1950s of an AEC Regal III of
MacBraynes outside Fort William station. Just visible in
the background is a Commer Commando from the
same operator, while a 'Black 5' blows off steam in the
station.
*All uncredited photographs are either from the Ian Allan
Library or were taken by the author*

Moreover new buses were needed. Operators had
had a tough time in the war and prewar buses which
under other circumstances would have been maturing
nicely had been run into the ground and needed
replacing. There was no shortage of passengers and
fleet replacement schemes got under way.

The standard British 1940s postwar bus had a front-
mounted diesel engine, with half-width cab alongside.
Double-deckers would almost without exception have
the entrance at the rear, either with an open platform
or maybe enclosed by platform doors. They would be
7ft 6in wide and 26ft long, typically with 56 seats,
although by the end of the 1940s dimensions had been
relaxed to 8ft wide by 27ft long, giving around 60
seats. Longer vehicles could be built on three axles
for higher capacity, though in practice only trolleybuses were available in this format after the war.
AEC, Guy and Leyland in particular had offered
three-axle motorbuses before the war, with limited
success, but none was offered on the home market in
postwar years. Trolleybuses were a different proposition, as the need to maximise the use of expensive
infrastructure meant that there was a requirement to
maximise passenger capacity. Single-deckers could
already be 27ft 6in on two axles.

Generally, only manufacturers of lighter vehicles,
such as Bedford, continued to offer petrol engines
after the war, and its OB chassis, a more refined
version of its wartime OWB, with a small petrol
engine in a conventional bonnet at the front, formed
the basis of many a 29-seat coach in this period.

However, passengers on single-deck routes may
well have noted major changes from the end of the

1940s; from 1946 underfloor-engined single-deckers
began to appear and these represented a large alter-
ation in the appearance of buses, with a full front and
entrance in an overhang ahead of the front axle.
BMMO was the first with its own vehicles (the S6),
while AEC brought out its Regal IV in 1949, with
refinements such as brakes and preselective gearbox
both operated by air pressure. Meanwhile, Leyland
had collaborated with body-builder Metro-Cammell
Weymann to go one stage further on its Olympic
model by eliminating the traditional separate chassis
at the same time. However, Sentinel is credited with
the first commercially available underfloor-engined
bus after the war. Sentinel was one of the last builders
of steam lorries, having produced particularly effective horizontal-engined vehicles during the 1930s and
similar technology (though using diesel power!) was
logically adapted to buses. Indeed, it offered only
horizontal engines in its postwar range, goods vehicles included.

The underfloor engine allowed a useful increase in
seating, up to 40, and later relaxation of the rules to
allow 30ft single-deckers on two axles increased this

to 44. There was also the potential for one-person operation, with passengers boarding alongside the driver, though this aspect was only to make an impact several years later; buses with more than 20 seats could only be one-man-operated by special dispensation from the Traffic Commissioners.

Leyland soon found resistance to chassisless, or integral, vehicles, and offered a separate chassis, the Royal Tiger, some of which were confusingly built with an identical MCW body to the Olympic. What these early underfloor-engined chassis did share was a very high unladen weight, and in the 1950s cost-saving became more significant as passenger numbers peaked and began their long, steady decline. Thus lighter-weight versions were produced; in the case of Leyland and AEC these were the Tiger Cub and Reliance respectively, which were both introduced in 1953. Ironically, the Reliance later developed into a premium, heavyweight coach chassis. There was also a chassisless Tiger Cub, or lightweight Olympic if you prefer, the Olympian, which sold in very small quantities on the home market.

Meanwhile, lighter-weight double-deckers were also built on new versions of existing chassis, and during the 1950s the traditional exposed radiator on double-deckers was often disguised by styled sheet metalwork, only Leyland continuing to offer exposed-radiator models well into the 1960s.

In 1954 Walsall Corporation had a batch of 30ft double-deck trolleybuses built on two axles and this paved the way to longer vehicles on two axles. Trolleybuses were subject to different rules and regulations to motorbuses (they were officially considered to be some sort of railway!) and thus it was sometimes possible to introduce new approaches on trolleybuses while they still could not be applied to motorbuses because of legal restrictions. Walsall's trolleybuses thus proved that a 30ft double-decker on two axles worked perfectly well and two years later 30ft two-axle double-deck motorbuses were legalised. The demand thus created was met in the main by lengthened versions of existing chassis. 36ft single-deckers were to be proven in the same way later in the decade; Glasgow introduced 10 34ft 5in 50-seat single-deck trolleybuses and by 1961 36ft single-deck motorbuses were authorised.

Going back to 1954, however, London Transport had commissioned a new generation of bus principally for the replacement of trolleybuses. Built by AEC and Park Royal (though prototypes involved other builders too) the legendary Routemaster had to be capable of carrying 64 passengers within the same laden weight as the 56-seat RT with no loss of comfort and with extra facilities for the driver.

Below:
In some ways a typical independent operator's fleet of the mid-1950s, though with rather superior depot accommodation compared with many. This 1955 shows the Worksop depot of Major's Coaches, just before it was taken over by East Midland. Visible are a late-Utility Guy Arab II and a pair of contrasting Dennis Lancet coaches.

The Routemaster achieved its aim despite a high level of comfort and power steering plus automatic transmission. Again chassisless construction was adopted, using an aluminium structure which not only proved very light but also immensely strong and durable. It retained traditional layout and was thus the ultimate development of the front-engined, halfcab bus — no further major developments were made to this type, although new versions of existing models and one complete new model — the AEC Renown — had yet to emerge.

The Renown, resurrecting the name of the prewar three-axle double-decker, was largely conventional, but had a low frame and dropped-centre rear axle to enable low-height double-deck bodywork to be built on it (though in fact some operators, such as Leicester and Nottingham used the low floor to create extra internal headroom instead). This was not a new concept; it had been developed as far back as 1949 by Bristol, which had been nationalised under the 1947 Transport Act and was thus permitted only to supply vehicles to the state sector, once orders in hand at the time the Act came into force had been fulfilled. Bristol sold its new bus as the Lodekka, and also allowed Dennis to build an open market version of it under licence as the Loline. Leyland had produced its own, not too satisfactory low-height bus, the Lowlander, which was built by Albion, since 1951 part of the growing Leyland group.

However, Leyland was pursuing a different avenue. Just as engines had been placed elsewhere on single-deckers Leyland developed a double-decker with a transverse rear engine. The first two prototypes were largely conventional in appearance, with the engine on the rear platform. However, before production began an integral version had been developed with MCW, with the engine in isolation behind the lower saloon and the entrance ahead of the front axle.

It went into production in 1958 as the Atlantean, by which time it could be built to 30ft length, and the decision had been taken to abandon the integral version and simply build a separate chassis, though MCW still built the bodywork for the first versions. Its main advantages were high seating capacity — up to 78 seats could be fitted in — while the driver could supervise boarding and unloading, even if he wasn't allowed at this stage to take the fares.

Daimler quickly followed with its Fleetline, which offered two advantages over the Atlantean; it could be fitted with low-height bodywork — on the Atlantean this could be achieved only by fitting a sunken side gangway upstairs towards the rear, reverting to the awkward pre-Lodekka arrangement, albeit not for the whole length of the bus, until it turned to Daimler and used the Fleetline gearbox in a low-height version. Its second advantage was that while Leyland insisted on fitting engines of its own make, Daimler could offer Gardner engines, which had been a favourite for bus work since diesel engines were first fitted to buses. This proprietary unit was very economical — despite little major design change since the early 1930s it took until the mid-1980s before any other manufacturer managed to match its fuel consumption — and was also very reliable and produced plenty of torque at low speeds, which was ideal for bus work.

At this stage no other manufacturer was pursuing such development in the bus world, although Guy tried a different approach from Leyland and Daimler.

Right:
New look for the 1970s. South Yorkshire PTE tried a variety of modern types on its 51 service; from left to right they are a Leyland Titan, an MCW Metrobus (both demonstrators), an East Lancs-bodied Leyland Atlantean, an East Lancs-bodied Dennis Dominator and a Van Hool-McArdle-bodied Ailsa.

Its Wulfrunian used a Gardner 6LX engine ahead of the front axle, with the entrance alongside and a staircase over the nearside front wheel. This was combined with other complexities, and its problems proved insurmountable. The weight imbalance was too great, especially given the sophistication of the front suspension and brakes, and as one of the classic flops of the bus world it brought Guy down with it.

The die was now cast, even if bus operators were expected to cope with a reduction in reliability. Tried and tested components which worked well in a conventional location, with plentiful natural air flow around them and mounted alongside the driver, where he could hear or feel if something was amiss, suddenly proved much less reliable when tucked away in a powerpack at the back of the bus. Although many operators stuck doggedly to the front-engined layout as long as possible, the industry was gradually persuaded that worse fuel consumption and much greater unreliability was a small cost to pay for fashion and a few extra seats!

However, one-person operation of double-deckers was legalised in 1966, which rather changed the equation. The first operator to take advantage of the new legislation was Brighton Corporation, which used conventional forward-entrance Leyland Titans, requiring the driver to turn round in his seat to serve passengers and giving him no ease in the physical job of driving to make up for his extra work load. Eastern National and Eastern Scottish tried a similar approach with Bristol Lodekkas. Most operators, however, recognised the importance of having the entrance placed opposite the driver if he was expected to relieve passengers of their fares as they boarded.

Bristol had now joined the move to rear engines with its VR, appearing in prototype form in 1966 with in-line engine on the offside. However, it changed horses, abandoning what could have been a very versatile design for the now-conventional arrangement of a transverse engine. By now Bristol had been liberated from the constraints to sell only to the state sector, as Leyland had taken a 25% shareholding in 1965, and this had enabled it to sell new products to all-comers. Its RE rear-engined single-decker was undoubtedly the most successful of a troublesome crop of new rear-engined single-deckers from the likes of Leyland, AEC and Daimler. These designs gave the advantage of a low entrance and high capacity, now that single-deckers could be built up to 36ft. This gave seating capacity on a par with double-deckers, at 53, and allowed for one-person operation before it could be applied to double-deckers.

AEC's foray into rear-engined double-deckers was shortlived; an intention to build five rear-engined Routemaster prototypes was commuted by Leyland and only one was built. It shared the basic structure of the Routemaster and used about 60% of standard Routemaster components. FRM1, as the one that was built was numbered, still exists as a museum piece, and many have a sneaking suspicion that it could have been a great success. Not all the lessons learned in building it were consigned to the dustbin, however, and it had at least some bearing on the later Leyland Titan. Internally it seemed rather better designed than other rear-engined types at the time, with a particularly neat interior and if it had proved to be as well-designed structurally as the Routemaster there seems little doubt that it could have been a winner. In all

deckers, built by the likes of Bedford and Ford. In 36ft form they could carry nearly as many passengers as a double-decker, yet were much cheaper to buy and, with their dependence on high-volume, medium-weight trucks for parts, they were cheap to run and maintain. They entered fleets of small independent operators which had traditionally used secondhand double-deck stock, though also appeared with major company operators in both the National Bus Company and Scottish Bus Group. One municipal operator, Maidstone, also standardised on Bedfords to replace its fleet of Leyland double-deckers.

Of more significance was the second-generation rear-engined single-decker, of which the principal example was the Leyland National. This was designed by Leyland in conjunction with the National Bus Company and embodied very strong, integral construction, which avoided the problem encountered with the earlier generation where conventional bodywork had tended to sag with the weight of the engine in the rear overhang. The Leyland National also had air suspension, paving the way to near universal adoption of this feature, giving not only a better ride but making for easier maintenance than conventional leaf springs. Other features were power steering and ergonomic design to the benefit of both driver and passenger. It was a highly standardised bus, with a very limited range of options — indeed at first they were supplied only in a choice of three plain colours, red, green or white. This was in stark contrast to the traditional way of building buses, which were more often than not a bespoke product for individual operators, and such an approach enabled it to be mass-produced, car-like, by semi-skilled labour in a brand new purpose-built factory in Workington, Cumbria. Some 7,000 Leyland Nationals were built from 1971 to 1984.

Leyland had gradually been expanding its dominance of the bus world. It had merged with ACV, an amalgamation of AEC, Crossley, Maudslay, Thornycroft and bus bodybuilders Park Royal and Roe in 1962, and its shareholding in Bristol was increased to 50% in 1969, by which time the rest of its shares were owned by the National Bus Company.

lines of British engineering there seem to be 'might-have-beens' which looks so promising. London instead went for the Fleetline for one-person operation, and while there was nothing particularly wrong with the Fleetline as a bus, by the time it had been hacked about to suit London's 'unique' requirements it was something of a disaster. One also suspects there was a certain death wish on it from the start in London — but we're getting a bit ahead of ourselves.

The 1968 Transport Act had a profound effect on the bus world. Its main effects were that the state-owned National Bus Company was formed, encompassing almost all the major company operators. Those which were part of the BET Federation had sold out to their state-owned THC counterparts a little earlier. The municipal operators in four major conurbations were amalgamated into Passenger Transport Executives, and to speed one-person operation the Government introduced a 25% capital grant, later increased to 50%, for new buses which met certain parameters, notably that they could be operated without a conductor. This spelt the end of the conventional double-decker, and by 1968 production ended of the Leyland Titan, AEC Regent and Routemaster, Daimler CVG6, Guy Arab (Guy had been taken over by Daimler and continued as a separate entity after its Wulfrunian disaster) and Bristol Lodekka.

As a result these well-built and reliable vehicles had a much shorter lifespan, in most cases, than they were designed for, and they were replaced by vehicles suitable for one-person operation. This brought about too an increase in popularity of lightweight single-

One of the most momentous events in the British automotive industry was the merger of what had become Leyland Motor Corporation since the ACV merger and what was then British Motor Holdings. Up to 1966 BMH had been BMC, but the takeover of Jaguar had brought about the change of title. Jaguar owned Daimler and Guy, so by now Leyland was becoming something of a monolith in the bus building industry.

Certain operators were dismayed at this situation, and other manufacturers were not slow to exploit it. Firstly came Scania, in conjunction with body-builder Metro-Cammell Weymann, which was concerned that Leyland's move to integral construction would rob it of any business. Its Metro-Scania was a direct rival to the Leyland National and while it sold in fairly small numbers a double-deck counterpart proved rather more of a serious rival. However, it was significant in that it was a toe-hold for overseas manufacturers which would soon lead to the virtual demise of UK manufacturers.

Dennis, which had pulled out of bus building in 1968 — and indeed had shown little enthusiasm for bus building for some years before that — was also encouraged to introduce a new rear-engined double-decker, the Dominator, which was intended as an alternative to the Daimler Fleetline which Leyland was in the process of phasing out, and this was later to lead to a whole range of products and set up Dennis as the last remaining British bus chassis manufacturer. The Dominator sold reasonably well, largely to municipal and PTE operators — South Yorkshire

PTE took to it, unusually with Rolls-Royce engines — and was later to spawn other models, notably the Falcon single-decker, which, with a rear horizontal Gardner engine was a sort of latter-day Bristol RE.

Meanwhile the coach business was largely in the hands of Leyland companies for the heavyweight market — notably the mid-engined Leyland Leopard and AEC Reliance — and Bedford and Ford for the lightweight, the former with a mid, vertical engine, the latter with a front engine though inclined to fit under the floor. They were soon joined by another importer, Volvo, with a similar but rather more sophisticated and powerful mid-engined heavyweight, the Swedish-built B58.

Volvo's Scottish importer, Ailsa Trucks, also saw potential for a simple, rugged front-engined double-decker, though with the entrance alongside the driver Guy Wulfrunian-style. It had several advantages over the ill-fated Wulfrunian; it retained conventional suspension and brakes, it used a semi-integral body by Alexanders to overcome structural difficulties and a small turbocharged Volvo engine. Such a power unit was at first regarded with disdain as not being 'man' enough for the job, but Volvo engineers knew their stuff and for the most part the engine confounded its critics. However, despite the dislike of rear engines the Ailsa did not sell in huge numbers outside Scotland. Perhaps it had come too late; by now engineers had got used to rear engines and the problems of early vehicles had been sorted out to a large extent.

Leyland intended to continue the rationalisation of

its range. The Leyland National had been seen as the way forward, with a perceived move to single-deckers. However, Leyland had misread the market and with one-person operation of double-deckers now perfectly feasible large operators moved back to double-deckers. Leyland's Project B15, which came to be known as Titan, was a sort of double-deck Leyland National; the concept was largely similar, a fully integral bus with air suspension, though independent at the front, and lots of sophistication. It was hit by major production problems and became essentially a London vehicle, large early orders for provincial centres going largely unfulfilled and never being repeated.

Just as the Titan entered production MCW had ended its relationship with Scania and began building a rival to the Titan, the Metrobus, using a Gardner engine and German Voith transmission. It was not so sophisticated as the Titan, but MCW was rather more successful at getting production under way and it sold more widely than the Titan. Moreover it could be produced as a separate underframe and was later bodied, albeit in fairly small numbers, by Alexander and Northern Counties. Plans for Titans to be built by Northern Counties for its parent Greater Manchester PTE came to nought.

Leyland also soldiered on with an ageing range of double-deck and coach chassis, the latter being outclassed now by foreign competition. The coach business was deregulated in 1980, and Leyland was only able to offer chassis which had evolved since the 1950s. Operators turned overseas for such features as air suspension and powerful turbocharged engines, often mounted at the rear to give better luggage accommodation and minimise noise intrusion into the saloon. UK bodybuilders had also fallen behind with styling, and it was overseas manufacturers which were the main beneficiaries of deregulation. Rather belatedly Leyland introduced the Tiger, with air suspension and a more powerful, turbocharged engine, and followed it with a stylish rear-engined integral, the Royal Tiger Doyen. This was the equal of anything the continental manufacturers could offer in terms of styling and comfort, but by now coach operators had lost faith in Leyland. It could not offer the same level of back-up on Continental work and there were doubts over build quality.

Meanwhile the major British express operator, National Express, called for a new high-floor rear-engined coach. Dennis and Duple responded with a coach version of the Falcon with Duple's high-floor Goldliner body. The Dennis was powered by a turbocharged Perkins V8. Most of Dennis's models at this time could be equated with vehicles of earlier generations; in this case the coach version of the Falcon was a sort of latter-day Daimler Roadliner; the Roadliner had not been one of Daimler's high points . . . Sadly National Express's timescale had been too tight to allow proper development, and while the Falcons went like the wind and were superbly comfortable, smooth and quiet there had been no time to get the bugs out of them. Failures which should have occurred on the test track and been ironed out thus occurred very publicly, in service, and almost cost Dennis its hard-won reputation.

On the double-deck front there was also a rethink at Leyland in the face of opposition to the Titan, and the same mechanical units were put into a chassis, though with a brand new front axle and suspension arrangement. It was able to take low-height bodywork, which the Titan wasn't, and it could be bodied by a range of manufacturers. After a slowish start the Olympian replaced the Atlantean, Fleetline and Bristol VRT and proved highly successful.

Meanwhile single-deck sales fell drastically and the Leyland National was reaching the end of the road. Bus deregulation was announced in a Transport Bill in 1984 (enacted as the 1985 Transport Act), bringing with it privatisation of the National Bus Company and with provision for other public sector operators to go private too.

This stifled all investment in large vehicles, for a number of reasons. Bus grants had been steadily phased out during the early 1980s, at a time when increasing European legislation on safety, accessibility and emissions was making buses ever more complex and therefore expensive. Subsidies for bus operations, which in many cases were substantial by 1990s terms, if not by Continental European terms, were cut back to the bare minimum and operators were also left in a state of uncertainty, with any profits likely to be creamed off by newcomers. The newcomers were coming in at the lowest possible cost using rolling stock cast off by larger operators reducing their fleet sizes, so they offered little hope to the bus manufacturers. And what money that was available was not being spent on new buses but on raising capital to buy bus companies either from public-sector owners or from other private-sector owners.

There was, however, a major move to van-based minibuses which were cheaper to buy and to run and could be used to open up areas inaccessible to large buses. The main bus builders found themselves unable to offer suitable products, though MCW was soon to come up with the integral 25-seat Metrorider. Deregulation killed the demand for large single-deckers and Leyland therefore took its time over introducing the replacement for the Leyland National, the Lynx, though it did sell reasonably well once introduced, boosted by large orders from West Midlands Travel, Badgerline and the West Riding Group.

As part of its privatising zeal the Government also wished to rid itself of British Leyland, which it had picked up during difficult phases in the 1970s. The cars, trucks and bus businesses were sold separately. General Motors, which owned Bedford, was inter-

Above:
The final flowering of the true British bus? Leyland's
last new model was the Lynx, an integral single-decker.
This one was built in 1990 for Preston Bus.
Michael H. C. Baker

ested, but it was unacceptable to have such a strategic interest as Land Rover owned overseas — ironic in view of the final outcome, which now finds it owned by BMW. GM wanted the truck business plus Land Rover, and its failure to gain it meant that it decided Bedford was unable to carry on alone — much investment was needed in new models which volumes looked unlikely to sustain — and closed it down.

There was a similar situation at MCW. In 1986 the Laird Group, which owned MCW, looked at the possibility of buying Leyland Bus, which could have made a strong, combined bus-building group. Ultimately, Leyland Bus was sold to its management in 1987, which sold it on to Volvo in the following year. Then at the end of 1992, having given many undertakings as to the bright future, Volvo closed Leyland as volumes were still down. It reopened its Irvine truck plant, where the Ailsa had been built, to bus production, revamped the Olympian as a pure Volvo product and built that and a new small single-decker, the B6, there.

Meanwhile the Laird Group decided not to continue sustaining losses at MCW, which it closed at the end of 1988, its model range passing to Optare, a relatively new bodybuilder which had been formed at the former Roe factory shut by Leyland in 1984.

Dennis, however, prospered. Its Javelin mid-weight coach was an innovative design and came in just at the right time to pick up sales from Bedford. Had GM invested in a new coach range it would not be unreasonable to surmise that it may have come out very much the same as the Javelin. Dennis repeated its success with a small rear-engined single-decker, the Dart, which was introduced at the 1988 Motor Show,

and production began in 1990. This was a spectacular success, as it was just the right size to take over from minibuses where they had developed traffic to the point where they were now too small and at the same time it was big enough to take over from full-sized single-deckers on routes where traffic was declining. By 1994 2,000 had been built. It used simple technology in an imaginative way to create a reasonably sophisticated bus, a formula used again for the full-sized rear-engined Lance. The Lance was well up to the standard of much more complex Continental-built vehicles for standards of comfort, performance and accessibility at much lower cost and with less to go wrong. It formed the basis of the first British sortie into a new European technology, the ultra-low-floor bus which aims to be the ultimate in accessibility.

At the time of writing, at the end of 1994, there were brighter signs on the horizon. Four of the emerging major bus groups had been floated on the stock exchange and were thus in a good position to raise cash. They and others are investing in buses again, in good quantities. But the British bus manufacturing base was decimated in the 1980s. Now only Dennis flies the flag as a truly British chassis manufacturer, though Volvo builds buses at Irvine and Optare still builds the MetroRider.

ACE/Ward

One of the delightful things about the British automotive industry is the way from time to time a small company will have a go at producing something which isn't otherwise available on the market. This is particularly so in the bus industry; numerous small companies have come and gone, leaving a legacy of an oddball vehicle here and there. Sadly they seldom have the staying power to survive, even if their ideas are good. They tend to be undercapitalised and have great difficulty in assuring potential users of their credibility.

ACE is the most recent example. It had some good designs, and like many such companies began life when an operator wanted a vehicle which nobody built. ACE, based in Huddersfield, began life as Ward Brothers. Wards had (indeed still has) a medium-sized coach business in Lepton, to the south of Huddersfield, and was particularly keen on Seddon Pennines with Perkins V8 engines. After Seddon stopped building such vehicles it started work in 1980 to build its own 36ft coach chassis with a mid-mounted Perkins V8, called the Dalesman. It was fitted in 1981 with a well-appointed Plaxton Supreme IV coach body. Engineer Keith Ward disliked power steering, not least for its effect on tyre wear, so the vehicle was built without that feature. It had a ZF six-speed synchromesh gearbox, which can be a tricky box in many well-established manufacturers' products, yet Wards managed a superb installation which worked extremely well.

Above:
The start of a new manufacturer. What was to become ACE began life as Ward, with this Perkins V8-powered mid-engined Dalesman C11-640 chassis. It had a Plaxton Supreme body and is seen on a cold day in the Pennines on a *Buses* road test.

Left:
A Perkins-engined ACE Puma of Huddersfield operator Abbeyways at a show in Renfrew. Bodywork is by Plaxton, the low-driver version of the Paramount 3200 body. Abbeyways had connections with ACE through managing director Steven Ives.
Sandy Macdonald

It bowed to pressure to fit power steering on production vehicles.

Its next project was another 'Seddon clone' the GRXI, a rear-engined service bus with a horizontal Gardner engine and SCG semi-automatic gearbox, very similar in many respects to the Seddon Pennine RU. Six were built in 1983 for Darlington Transport, and no further orders were received. Wards closed down in 1984 having built 18 chassis in total.

However, from the ashes arose a company called AEC (Albion Equipment Co), started by another Huddersfield coach operator, Steven Ives plus two of the Ward Brothers. It announced a range of three chassis, the Puma, Cheetah and Cougar, all using Perkins engines. Not surprisingly Leyland which had rights not only to the original AEC name but also to Albion, objected and it was quickly renamed ACE (Advanced Chassis Engineering). The Cheetah was the successor to the Ward Dalesman, but with a dropped driver position as was then fashionable, while the Puma was a short-wheelbase midicoach chassis, of which 12 were sold, one with a DAF DHT 8.25litre engine. The Cougar took longer to come on stream, and was a rear-engined 10m bus chassis with a ramped floor. Only two were built and the company closed down in 1992.

AEC

AEC, based in postwar years at Southall, Middlesex, was very much one of the 'giants' of bus manufacturing, having been established originally as the 'builder of London's buses' as it used to advertise itself.

After the war it essentially had two ranges, one for London and one for the provinces. Just before the war London's RT version of AEC's double-decker, the Regent, had seen the light of day and postwar production began quickly. The RT was ahead of the field with a powerful 9.6litre engine, air-operated prese-

lector gearbox, air brakes and a low bonnet line to give excellent visibility. Some 4,650 London RTs were built after the war until production ended in 1954.

The RT was also offered to provincial operators, but more conventional Regents were also offered, starting immediately after the war with a stop-gap Regent II, largely following on from prewar practice and built to a rather basic specification. The Regent III was available in various forms with a range of engines from 7.7 to 9.6 litres capacity, preselector, synchromesh or constant-mesh gearboxes and air or vacuum brakes. The bonnet line was higher than the RT, and a few operators specified concealed radiators in the 1950s. There was a parallel Regal single-deck version, which was successful as both a bus and a coach, spawning some very attractive coach versions especially once 30ft versions were legalised.

Before the war AEC had been experimenting with engine positions, and had built an underfloor-engined bus for Canada as well as underfloor-engined railcars for the Great Western Railway. Similar technology was embodied in the Regal IV introduced in 1949, with a standard preselector gearbox and air brakes. This formed the basis of either a bus or a coach and offered not only style but a higher seating capacity, albeit for a very substantial weight penalty over the front-engined Regals. A London version the RF, was built in 1951-53.

The commercial vehicle industry as a whole, and the bus industry in particular, became obsessed with weight saving in the 1950s as economies had to be introduced following the beginnings of a tail-off in passengers as car ownership grew. In AEC's case, following lightweight versions of the Regent III, a new lightweight range was introduced to supersede the earlier models. In 1953 came the Reliance, a lightweight underfloor-engined single-decker, following the realisation that underfloor-engined buses would not fall apart without a structure like the Forth Bridge under the floor. The same components could be had in a Park Royal-built integral, the Monocoach. An unsuccessful foray into an underfloor-engined double-decker, the Regent IV, showed there was no advantage to be gained from increasing the complexity of a double-decker at this stage, so the lightweight double-decker was the Regent V, which offered a stylish concealed radiator as standard.

Although conceived as lightweights both Regent V and Reliance grew into heavyweights in later life, the Reliance in particular turning out to be AEC's last chassis, metamorphosed into a sophisticated premium motorway coach by the time of its demise in 1979.

Meanwhile London Transport too was looking at increasing seating capacity within the same laden weight as an RT for trolleybus replacement, resulting in the classic Routemaster, of which prototypes appeared in 1954 and production began in 1958. This embodied many advanced features such as coil suspension, independent at the front, automatic transmission and power steering, arranged in two subframes built into an aluminium integral body structure by Park Royal. AEC built 2,873 of them, though some had Leyland engines, and in 1966 developed a rear-engined version, of which only one prototype was built.

Similar, though simplified, technology was adopted for a new provincial double-decker, the Bridgemaster, of which Crossley-bodied prototypes appeared in 1956. Production buses were bodied by Park Royal from 1958, using steel rather than the Routemaster's aluminium. It had a dropped-centre rear axle to enable low-height bodywork to be built without recourse to a sunken gangway upstairs. It was not one of AEC's more auspicious products and sold only 179.

In 1962 AEC sold out to archrival Leyland. It had taken over Crossley and Maudslay in 1948 to form Associated Commercial Vehicles, merged with Park Royal, which also owned Charles H. Roe, in 1949 and had taken over Thornycroft in 1961, and thus represented a substantial sector of the bus and commercial vehicle business. However, it was able to continue as a separate entity and still built its products at its Southall, Middlesex factory. Its last new double-decker was launched at this time, the Renown, which used AEC Regent V components in a low-height form, and provided a more conventional replacement for the Bridgemaster. About 250 Renowns were built.

Meanwhile a rear-engined single-decker was in development, the Swift. Although using AEC components the Swift was a product of the merger with Leyland, for the same chassis was also built with Leyland components as the Panther. It used the 8.25litre AH505 engine, though some had the bigger 11.3litre AH691 engine, also fitted to London's heavyweight version, the Merlin. Semi-automatic transmission was standard, though the Swift was available for rural use with a five-speed constant-mesh unit.

There was to be one further AEC; at the 1970 Commercial Motor Show an impressive rear-engined coach with a V8 engine appeared, the Sabre. It had a new ECW body, and although the chassis never got beyond prototype stage the body was reworked for the Bristol RE. By this time AEC was building only single-deckers; the Regent V and Routemaster had ended in 1968, and AEC had no new rear-engined bus to replace them. The Swift continued in production until 1975 and the Reliance, by now a premium heavyweight coach, far removed from the original concept, alone kept the AEC name going until this very popular marque was closed down in 1979. The final Reliances had 691 or even bigger 760 12.5litre engines with ZF six-speed gearboxes or semi-automatic transmission and were fine, high-speed motorway performers. They were superseded in the Leyland range by the less powerful and less refined Leopard, of which a special version with ZF gearbox was built to cater for the AEC market, though many AEC customers preferred to turn to Volvo or DAF.

Above:
A splendid scene in Leeds in about 1950 shows West Riding 74 (BHL 190), a Regent III with Roe centre-entrance bodywork passing a Leeds tramcar.

Below:
The single-deck version of the Regent III was the Regal III. Seen when new in 1949 is a Weymann-bodied example for East Midland.

Right:
The Regal III was also popular as a coach. This one has bodywork by Longford to a classic late-1940s style, and is seen in 1964 in service with West Riding. It was new in 1949 to Bullock & Sons, which was taken over by West Riding the next year.
J. Fozard

Centre right:
London Transport's own version of the Regal IV was the RF type, which was often to be found on the extremities of LT's operations. Seen in May 1962, still requiring a conductor and open front door, to keep the Metropolitan Police happy, this picture of RF421 in Shepperton High Street was taken from outside what, 32 years later, was to become the *Buses* editorial office, where much of this book was written!
Michael Dryhurst

Below:
The provincial version of the Regal IV made a superb, if very heavy, coach, with a quality of ride and noise levels, and ease of driving, which would rival many coaches built 30 years or more later. This one, for Scottish operator Northern Roadways, had Burlingham Seagull bodywork.

Above:
After AEC's heavyweight period came some lightweight designs, not least the Regent V. This Devon General bus had lightweight MCW Orion bodywork — and would also have featured a straight-through exhaust, giving a splendid sporty, rasping crackle. Behind is the old order, a rather heavier Weymann-bodied Regent III.
Kevin Lane

Centre left:
AEC's lightweight single-decker was the Reliance, though this was to grow in size and weight over the years. Many a BET company had Reliances with this style of bodywork in the late 1950s/early 1960s, built by a variety of builders. This Yorkshire Woollen District one had Park Royal bodywork and was new in 1960.

Bottom left:
This Reliance was a late survivor with Chiltern Queens and is seen at Reading in 1975. Unusually it carried the body from the one-off Dennis Pelican.
Kevin Lane

Top:
Though Burlingham's Seagull body of the 1950s was a classic, the Seagull 60 was less universally acclaimed. This new one on an AEC Reliance for Scottish Omnibuses in 1961 looks handsome enough, though.

Above:
Also with Scottish Omnibuses is a pair of AEC/Park Royal Monocoaches seen at St Andrew Square in Edinburgh in December 1954.

Above:
The AEC/Park Royal integral Bridgemaster was not an outstanding success. This one began life with South Wales but is photographed with Yorkshire Woollen District in Dewsbury in 1969.
Michael Fowler

Left:
The Routemaster proved remarkably enduring; it was introduced in 1954 and was still in service in 1994 when photographed at Victoria. This London Central bus is the 30ft long version, RML2345, as refurbished a year or two earlier.

Right:
Much lamented was the fact that the rear-engined Routemaster project never got off the ground — though had thousands of them been built they may have been despised as the bus that ousted the Routemaster! Who knows? FRM1 was originally built with no opening windows, though after it caught fire the opportunity was taken to fit some opening windows when it was repaired and returned to service. It is seen on the 76.
K. Pratt

Below:
After the Bridgemaster failed to catch on AEC introduced the Renown on a separate chassis. North Western was a major customer, with this Park Royal body which was rather better proportioned than that for the Bridgemaster. 1964-built 119 is seen on North Western's parking ground behind Mersey Square in Stockport in the company of a Marshall-bodied Bristol RESL.

Above:
Though it began life as a light-weight the Reliance developed into a premium heavyweight motorway coach. This Plaxton Supreme-bodied coach of Premier Travel makes an imposing sight as it leaves Drummer Street bus station in Cambridge in 1982. Next to it is a slightly older Reliance with Plaxton Panorama Elite bodywork.
Kevin Lane

Centre left:
Though not considered one of AEC's finest, the London heavy-weight version of the Swift, the Merlin, put in useful service on the intensive Red Arrow network.
A. Fox collection

Below left:
AEC's last new model was the Sabre with a rear-mounted V8-800 engine and a new body by ECW. The body was adapted for the Bristol RE, though the Sabre never entered production. The one-off vehicle, seen at the 1970 Commercial Motor Show at Earls Court, nevertheless saw a full service life.

Ailsa

Throughout this book you will find references to the 1948 Commercial Motor Show, which was highly significant in that several postwar models made their debut there. Another significant show in postwar years was the 1973 Scottish Motor Show, at which three psvs were seen for the first time. One was the Seddon Pennine VII, a thoroughly British, very solid chassis, but the other two were something different in that they introduced some foreign content and represented different ways forward for the double-decker. One was the Metro-Scania Metropolitan; the other was the Scottish-built Ailsa.

Ailsa was based at a former munitions factory near the Ayrshire coast at Irvine — almost in sight of the island of Ailsa Craig whence came its name. It had been set up to import Volvo trucks into Britain in 1967, and in 1971 started the Ailsa Bus Company initially to import B58 coach chassis into Britain.

However, in 1973 it announced an unusual Volvo-engined psv. At this stage rear-engined chassis had become universal in terms of production, although not in the affections of engineers. The bugs had not yet been ironed out of them, and problems were exacerbated by shortages of spare parts and long delivery times. The engineers hankered after something simpler, and thus the Ailsa was born.

Guy had previously shown how not to build a front entrance bus with a front engine and never recovered from its Wulfrunian fiasco. Mechanically the Ailsa was much simpler, with no independent air suspension or disc brakes to cloud the issue. The other problem was the space taken up by the Gardner

'lump', which Ailsa overcame by using a compact, high-revving turbocharged Volvo TD70 6.7litre engine which pushed out a highly creditable 190bhp, even if the torque levels were rather lower than most people liked for bus work. This unit was immediately viewed with suspicion by engineers; as Midlander, himself an engineer, reported in *Buses* when the Ailsa was announced, ' . . . 6.7litre swept capacity is likely to be too small for a double-deck design with an unladen weight of just over 9 tons'. This was the accepted logic of the time, though in fact that engine was used in heavier lorry applications and proved very much more capable, reliable and economical than anyone first thought. And being so small, it didn't take up as much room on the platform and in the cab as the Gardner had done on the Guy.

The Ailsa had an unusual design of perimeter underframe — a bit like that on a Bristol Lodekka, only more so, and was designed to be integrated into an Alexander body structure. The rest of the design was well-proven in the main, with a mid-mounted SCG gearbox and Kirkstall front axle with ZF power steering, though the rear axle was a drop-centre hub-reduction unit made by Hamworthy, which was perhaps a little more exotic than most. Despite the ability this created for low-height variants all bar one was built to full height. Indeed the Hamworthy axle was to be something of a weak point on it, and when a Mark III version was introduced in 1980 a conventional Volvo rear axle was substituted.

Being built in Scotland and being mechanically straightforward it was not surprising that the Scottish Bus Group should be a major customer, and the first big order was for 40 for Alexander Fife. Thereafter it

Right:
An Alexander-bodied Ailsa in service with West Midlands PTE at Oldbury in 1982.
Kevin Lane

remained primarily a Scottish vehicle, as Strathclyde PTE and Tayside also took in large numbers. However, there were significant customers in England too; West Midlands PTE took 50 in 1975, after three pre-production vehicles, and South Yorkshire PTE took 62 with Irish-built Van Hool-McArdle bodywork of particularly striking appearance in 1976.

The Mark II version came out in 1977, with detail modifications and the choice of Voith or Allison transmission as options to the standard SCG, and in 1980 the Mark III was introduced. Originally the Mark III was to have been marketed as a Volvo B55, though it was decided to revert to the name Ailsa. However, there is much confusion around this period as to whether one should refer to Volvos or Ailsas! An air suspension option came with the Mark III. New body options came in in about 1980 too, with Greater Manchester taking some late Mark IIs with Northern Counties bodies, Tayside had both Northern Counties and East Lancs while Derby City Transport and Strathclyde PTE each had two with Marshall bodywork.

The last new model to emerge from Ailsa was the Citybus. This used an Ailsa-style perimeter frame but with Volvo B10M mechanical parts, ie a mid-mounted 9.6litre horizontal engine, SCG gearbox and full air suspension. The prototype was bodied by Marshall for Strathclyde PTE. However, when production began in 1983 the Citybus was sold as a Volvo, and as volumes were small at first it was soon decided to offer a special version of the standard B10M, built in Sweden, as the Citybus instead of the Ailsa-built version. The Ailsa plant was used by Volvo for lorry manufacture and bus production was taking up valuable space where much larger numbers of lorries could be built. Ailsa production ended in 1985 with 40 B55s for Indonesia; the last British ones were built the previous year for Strathclyde PTE. Just over 1,000 had been built, nearly half of them for Scottish consumption, and no fewer than 321 went to Indonesia. Although thought-of as almost as an 'SBG special' in fact Scottish Bus Group had only 192 of that total, a figure which both Strathclyde and Tayside came close to matching. The Irvine factory then concentrated on lorries, but by hook or by crook is both nearly first and last in this book!

Albion

Albion was based in Scotstoun, near Glasgow, and was not exactly a mainstream bus builder, though it enjoyed some popularity in Scotland — notably with Glasgow Corporation — while in England Red & White also favoured the marque.

Its Venturer CX19 double-decker had entered production just before the war and recommenced production in 1946, with the options of Albion's own diesel or, surprisingly, petrol engines or the Gardner 6LW. It was the only postwar double-decker to offer a petrol engine, though in practice the only ones built were a 1948 export order to South African Railways; Albion sold strongly in territories such as South Africa and Australia. An updated CX37 with a more powerful Albion diesel engine superseded it in 1947. Glasgow Corporation was the main customer for the postwar Venturer, with 138 delivered between 1947 and 1953.

The single-deck equivalent was the Valiant, which

Below:
Albion was not a mainstream choice of vehicle for company operators outside Scotland, though Red & White was something of an exception. One of its Valkyrie CX19s with Lydney bodywork stands at Chepstow.
M. A. Sutcliffe

was built largely as a coach. However, Albion also had quite a reputation for its lighter-weight products, and offered a four-cylinder half-cab single-decker, the Valkyrie CX9, although the CX13 version offered either Albion's six-cylinder engine as fitted to the Valiant or the Gardner 5LW.

The lightest Albion single-decker was the Victor, intended largely for rural work and lightweight coaching. The first postwar version, the FT3AB, had a four-cylinder Albion petrol engine but the more popular FT39, introduced in 1948, had a four-cylinder diesel.

Albion ceased heavyweight production for the home market in 1951, and later that year was taken over by Leyland. On the home market it then concentrated on lightweights, after a very heavy underfloor-engined single-decker with a horizontally-opposed eight-cylinder engine, the KP71NW, got nowhere. In 1955 it launched a much smaller underfloor-engined chassis, the Nimbus, which was a midibus before its time. A larger model in 1957 was the Aberdonian, which again followed the lightweight theme; by this stage Leyland had launched its lightweight Tiger Cub and the Aberdonian used similar mechanical

Left:
More typical of the Victor, with exposed radiator, was this one for a Gloucestershire operator, Jenkins.

Centre left:
The Albion Aberdonian was effectively a lightweight version of the Leyland Tiger Cub. Manchester Corporation was an unusual operator to take the type with Seddon bodywork.

Below:
Bournemouth operator Charlie's Cars was a keen Aberdonian user. This one, bought after Charlie's Cars was taken over by Shamrock & Rambler, had Harrington Cavalier bodywork and is seen at Victoria Coach Station in July 1960.
Gavin Booth

components, though with a typically tuneful five-speed Albion constant-mesh gearbox which also came to be offered in the Tiger Cub, and this weighed in at 17cwt less even than the Tiger Cub. Again it sold reasonably well in Scotland, though one unusual English customer was Manchester Corporation, which added to this unusual move by having them bodied by Seddon. Other customers included Venture of Consett and the Ulster Transport Authority, which took 57. Like other Albions it was also something of a success on the export market.

A bigger Victor was announced in 1959; this was aimed at the market dominated by the Bedford SB, for a 41-seat front-engined forward control light-weight coach.

While Albion's range was kept separate from that of Leyland — although several Leyland Titans and

Above:
The Nimbus was a small light-weight bus chassis; Halifax Joint Omnibus Committee had a batch of 10 in 1963 with attractive Weymann 31-seat bodywork. 258 squeezes through Heptonstall, where its diminutive dimensions were probably more appreciated than its diminutive four-cylinder engine, in 1964.
Philip Torcliff

Centre right:
The Nimbus was known as a bus, but also appeared with coach body-work; this 29-seat Plaxton body makes for an attractive small coach. It operated for Maurice Watson Tours of Huntington, Yorkshire.
A. Hustwitt

Bottom right:
The Lowlander was a low-height version of the Leyland PD3. No attempt was made to lower the cab, resulting in a bizarre appearance more often than not. Alexander made no attempt to disguise this odd arrangement on its bodywork, which adorns this East Midland example.
Michael Fowler

Atlanteans for Glasgow carried Albion badging — Leyland used the Albion factory to produce a low-height version of the PD3, which was marketed as the Albion Lowlander. It was rather a late entrant to this market, in 1961, and appears to have been something of a knee-jerk reaction to the AEC Bridgemaster and Dennis Loline. Whilst it had a low chassis frame and dropped-centre rear axle the front end was pure PD3, leading to a rather bodged arrangement involving raised seats at the front upstairs to give the driver adequate headroom. Most were sold in Scotland, where 197 went to the Scottish Bus Group, but others sold to Ribble, East Midland, Yorkshire Woollen and Southend Corporation.

Albion's last home-market effort was the Viking, introduced in 1963 with a Leyland O.370 engine at the front opposite the entrance, and two years later the VK55 version had the same driveline but mounted in-line at the rear, principally for the Scottish Bus Group and for export. The Viking and similar Clydesdale continued for export until the 1980s, though latterly badged as Leylands.

Alexander

Walter Alexander was — and still is — well-known as a bus bodybuilder. However, it did have one dabble into a fully-integral vehicle in the 1970s. This was its S-series midibus, a 27-seater which entered production conveniently around the time Seddon stopped building the 4.236, often credited as being the first true midibus. The A-series was a more conventional large minibus design, however, rather than a scaled-down 'big bus'.

Alexander's main factory is at Falkirk, although it serves mainly the Irish market (both sides of the border) from its Alexander (Belfast) factory at Mallusk to the north of Belfast. This factory also tends to produce mini and midibuses, and was chosen to build the integral S-series. It was based on the Ford A-series, which offered some potential for a 27-seat bus but had rather a high frame, hence Alexander's decision to build it in integral form with a lower floor level than Ford could offer. The prototype emerged in November 1974 and did a demonstration round of various operators. The 7m long body had deep windows and a roof line not dissimilar to the Seddon, though with a very utilitarian front end which did it no favours. A more stylish front and rear were designed by Ogle for production models. They were based on the A0609 version of the A-series, with the Ford six-cylinder 3.6litre 87bhp diesel engine and offered a choice of Turner manual gearbox or Allison automatic.

Had it arrived 10 years later it would have sold like hot cakes, but the industry had only limited use for small vehicles at this stage. Nevertheless it sold tolerably well. The first were a batch of eight 23-seaters for West Midlands PTE at the end of 1975, and one was shown at the Scottish Motor Show that year. Other early customers were Grampian and National Bus Company, which had small numbers for Eastern Counties, Southdown and Hants & Dorset. Central SMT bought two in 1980 and took an earlier demonstrator.

Below:
National Bus Company took a number of the Alexander S-type integral minibus, based on Ford A-series parts. Western National 3 began life with Southdown.
Martin Curtis

Atkinson

Ever since man first learned the noble art of putting diesel engines into buses there has been a great desire for those diesels to be manufactured by Gardner. The problem was that to develop a diesel engine was an expensive business so most manufacturers which built their own engines insisted on fitting those engines to their chassis to keep the volumes up. When it came to the new rash of underfloor-engined single-deckers after the war the clear leaders in the field were AEC and Leyland — who would fit only their own engines, though there were a few Gardner-engined AEC Regent V double-deckers. Bristol fitted Gardners in its underfloor-engined buses, but these were not available on the general market.

North Western Road Car Co had been a keen Bristol user until sales became limited to the state sector, and would have liked a Gardner-engined single-decker with conventional transmission. Thus nearby lorry manufacturer Atkinson, of Walton-le-Dale, Preston, introduced such a chassis, the Alpha PM745H with an underfloor Gardner 5HLW horizontal five-cylinder engine and five-speed constant-mesh gearbox. This was followed by a PM746H, which was similar but with the more powerful Gardner six-cylinder 6HLW and a lightweight PL744 with the four-cylinder 4HLW engine. North Western and Lancashire United were major customers, taking 19 and 40 respectively, but smaller operators also took small numbers while Venture of Consett amassed a fleet of 24.

In 1954 Atkinson branched out into double-deckers, offering two PD746 models, largely conventional half-cab, front-engined vehicles, available with either manual or semi-automatic transmission. In the event only one of the latter was built, for the Stalybridge, Hyde, Mossley & Dukinfield board (it is preserved in the Manchester Museum of Transport), which had bought two PL745 single-deckers the previous year and had another two in 1955 and three in 1959. Production largely fizzled out around 1955, though penny numbers were built in the following years culminating with three single-deckers with modern Marshalls bodywork for Sunderland in 1963, the first for more than four years.

There was also a lorry-derived 30ft front-engined single-deck chassis with the Gardner 4LW engine, the L644LW EXL, which was intended primarily for export, though Sunderland had two with Roe bodywork and Carruthers, Dumfries, had a 27ft 6in version with Plaxton bus bodywork.

Altogether Atkinson built 117 psv chassis for the UK between 1950 and 1963, 100 of them by the end of 1955.

Austin

Although Austin was a very large builder of light-weight commercial vehicles it was never a major force in the bus industry. Its main passenger model, built from 1947 to 1950 was the CX, which was very similar to Bedford's rather better-known OB, with a six-cylinder, 3.5litre (later increased to four-litre) petrol engine in a conventional bonnet ahead of the driver, styled in a similar fashion to the Bedford. Indeed the type was sometimes referred to as the 'Birmingham Bedford'. It was essentially a small coach model, suitable for vehicles of around 29 seats and found some popularity amongst coach operators.

There was also a forward-control version, the CXB, which Mann Egerton fitted with an attractive coach body, immediately identifying the vehicle as an Austin with a front grille similar to contemporary goods vehicles and even having some resemblance to that on the A30 car.

Later generations of Austin light vans, such as the J2, also appeared as the basis of minibuses, notably with bodywork by Martin Walter. The last Austin-badged psvs, also badged Morris, were the 440EA, which was sold notably with 19-seat Ascough Clubman bodywork, built in Ireland, and the 550FG, which formed the basis of a small, 24-seat coach from 1969, though by 1971 both were being sold as Leyland Redlines.

Above:
Coach versions of the Atkinson Alpha were rather more rare. This PM746H, new in 1955, had Plaxton bodywork for Bracewells (Feather Group) of Colne, an enthusiastic Atkinson user which bought nine in four years.

Left:
Austin often built coaches in association with Kenex, which built the body on this 1948 CXB. The grille was of a style fitted to a number of Austin vehicles, cars included, at this time.

Above:
The 1¹/₂ ton Austin van was very common in the 1950s
as the basis of Royal Mail vans, ice cream vans,
laundry vans etc etc. This one, for Micro Coaches,
Bristol, had an attractive Reading coach body and was
built in 1956.

Below:
The 152 was also a very common type of vehicle in
various guises. This version was the Omnicoach, with
a 1,489cc, 42bhp petrol engine. 'Winking indicators
and tubeless tyres are included in the standard specification; heater and radio are optional extras' says the
Austin press release, dated 31 August 1960, which
accompanied the photograph. The Omnicoach was
available in 10-seat and 13-seat versions and formed
the basis of the first postbuses.

BMMO

The Birmingham & Midland Motor Omnibus Co Ltd, better known as Midland Red, was remarkable amongst British bus operators in that it built most of its own buses. Prewar they were known as SOS, but after the war they were known as BMMO.

Its prewar designs had also been sold to other operators such as Northern General and Trent, but after the war it built buses in its Carlyle Road Works at Edgbaston in Birmingham solely for its own use. Though Midland Red at the time was the biggest company operator, running just short of 2,000 buses in the 1950s and 1960s, one might still have thought that the scope for development of buses on such a small scale was limited. In actual fact BMMO's products were quite remarkable for their innovation, successfully using techniques which would even today be considered avant-garde. Nor did the company take the easy option by using proprietary components; it even built its own diesel engines.

Its first postwar double-decker to enter production was largely conventional. This was the D5, which followed on from a prototype built during the war, the REDD (rear-entrance double-decker, as opposed to the FEDD forward-entrance double-deckers which had been built before the war), which was later redesignated D1. Both used BMMO's K-type eight-litre six-cylinder engine and constant-mesh gearbox. The first 100 D5s were built in 1949 and another 100, designated D5B, came the next year. They were bodied by Brush to a distinctive style, using four-bay

construction, and an innovation was the use of a full-width bonnet and concealed radiator.

The next BMMO double-decker was the D7, of which 350 were built between 1953 and 1957. The D7 was bodied by Metro-Cammell and had an altogether tidier, smoother appearance than the D5. In keeping with the spirit of the age they were rather lighter than the D5s, though mechanically similar, and had seven more seats.

However, the greatest innovation in the early postwar years was in single-deckers. Rather surprisingly Midland Red had been able to continue

development work during the war and converted four buses which had been built as rear-engined single-deckers to underfloor engine, using a horizontal version of the K-type engine. As a result it was able to get ahead of the field and introduce its mid-under-floor-engined S6 as early as 1946.

Of even greater interest was the S5 prototype, which used similar components but in an integral, chassisless form, certainly an innovation at that time. However, the development was put on the back burner for a time and production was concentrated on vehicles with separate chassis, the S8, an 8ft wide version of the S6, coming in 1948, and an updated S9 in 1949-50. One hundred of each were built, followed by 156 S10s, again broadly similar, and 44 S12s which were built to the new 30ft length, allowing

seating capacity to be increased to 44, in 1950-51. The S10s were later extended to the same size. Meanwhile parallel coach models were built, the main mechanical difference being the use of a five-speed overdrive gearbox, though with more stylish body-work. Finally 99 S13s came in 1952, most of them dual-purpose.

The next major development was the S14. The prototype for this highly-innovative design was effectively the 100th S13, built in 1953. Mechanically it followed on from previous designs, with that horizontal K-series 8-litre engine, although a Hobbs automatic gearbox was fitted whereas production buses retained the four-speed constant-mesh unit. It was of integral construction with rubber suspension all round, independent at the front, and hydraulically-actuated disc brakes. It weighed in at under five tons unladen, remarkable for a bus of such technical innovation with a heavyweight driveline. As a result only single rear tyres were necessary.

The die was now cast for future BMMO production; integral construction, lightweight materials, independent front suspension and disc brakes were all to become hallmarks of the marque. The S14 was built from 1956 to 1958, during which time 219 entered service, along with 97 of the similar but more luxurious S15s, the last of which were built in 1962. But the most glamorous S14 spin-off was undoubtedly the C5 family of coaches, which included the impressive CM5 and CM5T motorway coaches. These legendary vehicles with possibly the most handsome styling of any BMMO product really captured the imagination by being ready for motorway work from the first day of the M1, and using a turbocharged version of the K-type engine and overdrive gearbox to reach reported speeds of 100mph. BMMO apparently had wanted something even more spectacular, and had tried to persuade the Ministry of Transport to relax the regulations to allow 45ft-long vehicles with 60 seats, and even converted an S8 to that length to press home the point. It was unsuccessful in this particular endeavour.

Subsequent BMMO models developed the same theme. Once regulations were relaxed to allow 36ft long vehicles the larger S16 was introduced in 1962, but shared the same mechanical components as the smaller S14 and S15, with which it compared unfavourably, so only 50 were built.

Meanwhile BMMO had introduced a new double-decker, the D9, in 1958. This employed similar techniques to the S14 and in many ways can be likened to the Routemaster, with its integral construction and independent suspension, though initially had disc brakes until these proved troublesome on a double-decker. A new 10.5litre version of the K-type engine had been developed for it, coupled to semi-automatic transmission. The other unusual feature was the set-back front axle, though a traditional half-cab layout was retained, giving the D9 a unique appearance. In 1960 BMMO went one stage further with its D10, which, like single-deckers, put the engine on the side under the floor and had the entrance ahead of the front axle. However, to keep the floorline low the crankcase was at the nearside of the vehicle, with the cylinders inboard, under the gangway. Two were built, one with a second door and staircase at the rear. However, the underfloor-engined double-deck concept was then to lie fallow for more than 20 years. However, BMMO went on to build 344 D9s before production ended in 1965.

Later single-decker designs also used the 10.5litre engine and semi-automatic transmission, resulting in a new breed of 36ft motorway coach, the CM6, and various single-deck designs, the S17, which was essentially the S16 with a bigger engine and semi-automatic transmission, S21, S22 and S23 which used a similar body structure to the CM6, though with bus styling, and brought BMMO production to an end in 1970 when National Bus Company had taken over Midland Red. By now larger numbers of standard Daimler Fleetlines and Leyland Leopards were entering service and these were considered a more practical way forward, especially as it was becoming more difficult to find suitable craftsmen to build the vehicles. The S21-23 classes together numbered 143 vehicles.

Left:
Midland Red 3694, built in 1950, was the prototype BMMO S13. It was bodied by Brush and was one of the first 30ft vehicles in the fleet. The conductor stands back deferentially to allow his rural passengers to board in a rather idyllic 1950 scene.

Top:
The S14 and S15 were the first production integral BMMOs, which also featured rubber suspension and disc brakes. This is an S15, the more luxurious, dual purpose version.

Above:
The first 36ft BMMOs were the S16 type, which had the same mechanical units as the 30ft S14 and S15 and were thus rather underpowered. This one is seen in Bearwood.
Patrick Kingston

Left:
One of the later BMMO designs was the S22, of which one is seen in Coventry on the X94 to Wellington in January 1968.
T. W. Moore

Centre left:
One hundred D5s were built with Brush bodywork in 1949/50.

Below:
Stuck in rush-hour traffic in Coventry, with plenty of Coventry Transport Daimlers in the background, is a BMMO D7. Midland Red had 200 D7s, with Metro Cammell bodywork, in 1954-57.
T. W. Moore

Above:
BMMO's last double-decker to go into full production was the integrally-built D9; a 1966 example is seen in Leamington on a local service.
T. W. Moore

Right:
Possibly the most revolutionary BMMO double-deck design was the D10, which resembled the D9 but had an underfloor engine to give a front entrance. Only two were built (the other had an additional door and staircase at the rear, though was later rebuilt as a single-door bus) and they were the first successful underfloor-engined double-deck designs.
K. D. Jubb

Above:
A typical postwar Beadle integral. This one, for Bristol, had Morris Commercial running units, but the same body style appeared on a variety of different bases, including Sentinel.

Beadle

John C. Beadle (Coachbuilders) Ltd of Dartford was in the ascendancy for a fairly short period after the war. Its great stock-in-trade was taking components from prewar buses and building them into its own patented all-alloy integral construction as single-deck buses or coaches. It started with four 33-seat proto-types built between 1945 and 1947, using respectively Commer, Leyland Cub, Bedford and Dennis Ace components, with Gardner 4LK engines in the Leyland and Dennis. Its first order was for 24 Leyland Cubs for Lincolnshire Road Car, while 12 vehicles were built on Morris Commercial parts in 1949/50 for Bristol, Hants & Dorset, Western National, West Yorkshire and United. However, the majority used components from prewar Leyland Titan TD4/TD5 and Tiger TS7/TS8 or AEC Regents and Regals for major operators not very far from its home ground, such as Maidstone & District, East Kent and Southdown, with smaller numbers for operators such as East Yorkshire, Yorkshire Traction and Yorkshire Woollen. Not just secondhand parts were used; 50 new Bedford OBs were built into Beadle structures in 1948/49 for Tilling-group operators. Altogether it built around 400 buses in this way, in addition to conventional bodies on chassis.

Beadle began to adapt its integral structure in other ways as early as 1948, when it could lay claim to having the only underfloor, horizontal-engined vehicle at the 1948 Commercial Motor Show, quite an achievement when big guns such as Leyland and AEC were beavering away at similar designs. In this case its integral structure had been adapted to fit Sentinel (qv) running units, the first of 26 Beadle/Sentinel combinations to be built over the following years.

In 1954 Beadle introduced a new integral model, again with an underfloor engine. Unlike the mainstream manufacturers, which used horizontal versions of existing vertical engines Beadle used an engine which had been designed as a horizontal engine from the start, the Commer TS3 two-stroke. This remarkable unit, which became well-known in Commer lorries, had three cylinders, each with two horizontally-opposed cylinders, to produce a highly respectable 105bhp from only 3.26litres. A coach version, the OE Mk II, followed in 1956. Altogether Beadle built 141 such Commer-based vehicles until production ceased in 1957, for which Devon General, Southdown, Yorkshire Woollen, PMT and Smiths of Wigan were significant customers. Beadle also produced smaller models, the Canterbury coach and Thanet bus, which were sold under its own name but were in fact based on modified Karrier Bantam chassis, with the option of either Commer TS3 diesel or Rootes petrol engines.

Beadle is now known as a motor dealer in North Kent.

Bedford

As the British commercial vehicle arm of American automotive manufacturer General Motors, Luton-based Bedford had established itself in the prewar years as a competent manufacturer of small, light-weight, normal-control coaches. It began production in 1931 and was the only manufacturer entitled to build single-deckers during the war. It had launched its petrol-engined OB in 1939, a slightly larger version of the earlier WTB, with a new front end and usually bodied with a Duple body to a design which was to become very familiar after the war, albeit with a few alterations. The war quickly interrupted production, but it resumed as the Utility version, the OWB, in 1942, and more than 3,000 had been built by September 1945.

Postwar OB production began a month later, and the type quickly established itself as the standard lightweight coach, operated by thousands of small coach operators — though bus versions were also built. Typically it had Duple's Vista body, with 29 seats, of which the first appeared in March 1946, though there were plenty of other builders for it. The OB retained the semi-normal-control layout of its prewar predecessor, and also retained the 3.5litre petrol engine, which produced 72bhp but was usually known by its RAC rating as a 28hp unit. It was 24ft long and had a gross vehicle weight of 7tons 3cwt. Some bodybuilders, such as Yeates and Burlingham, converted chassis to forward-control. Production continued until 1950, when it was replaced by the larger and heavier forward-control SB, by which time 7,200 had been built for the home market, and several thousand more were exported.

Bedford also built a comparable range of goods vehicles, and to confuse matters a small number of OBs were built for non-psv use while some of the goods chassis, such as the OLAZ, were bodied as buses which were visually very similar to the OB.

Though production ended in 1950 many survived into the era of preservation and there has been something of a renaissance of the OB for continued service over the last decade or so.

If the OB had been the standard British independent coach during the late 1940s, the SB became the standard British coach for the next decade. It was a front-engined chassis but of larger dimensions than the OB and was forward control. When introduced in 1950 it was intended as a 33-seater, but grew to the typical independent operator's 41-seater by 1956. It was also offered with a petrol engine, a 4.9litre unit of similar design to the OB's 3.5litre engine, though a diesel version with a 5.5litre Perkins R6, the SBO (O for oil engine) was introduced in 1953. The Perkins was later replaced by Bedford's own 330. The SB had a number of rivals, such as the Ford Thames, Commer Avenger and later the Albion Viking, but remained Bedford's sole passenger model for the 1950s and was by far the most popular vehicle of its genre, as a cheap, lightweight, simple and very effective chassis suitable for most small coach operators' use. It was still available, as the NJM, up to the end of Bedford production in 1986, though in latter years it was more likely to be specified for military use than for passenger work. It sold in excess of 50,000 units, including export to very many territories.

Below:
Contrasting Bedfords in the Cedar Coaches fleet, also based in Bedford. Nearer the camera is a Plaxton Paramount-bodied YNT, and next to it a classic OB, a type still able to give sterling service.
Kevin Lane

Bedford was to remain faithful to the front-engine concept with its next generation, introduced from 1962. In that year it returned to the 29-seat concept with its VAS, though now in forward-control form, as a sort of diminutive SB. It too was available with a choice of petrol or diesel engines and remained in Bedford's catalogue to the end. It was never to prove as popular as the SB, being rather more specialist, but found a rôle as a useful vehicle for feeder work for tour operators, welfare work, airline crew work and the like. It too remained in production to the end, as the PJK.

The next year Bedford produced its first vehicle suitable for 36ft coaches, the VAL, and this adopted an imaginative approach. Rather than developing axles specifically for a 36ft coach Bedford, which relied heavily on truck components in its psv range, instead used three lighter-weight axles from its truck range, in a 'Chinese six', or twin steer, set up, with diminutive wheels and, unusually at that time, power steering. The engine was mounted at the front, though ahead of the axles which were set back to allow a front entrance. At first the 6.54litre Leyland 400 was standard, although a new Bedford diesel, the 7.6litre 466, was introduced in the VAL70 in 1966. Duple, which since the days of the OB, had been most readily identified as the 'standard' coachbuilder on Bedford chassis, introduced a stylish new body for it, the Vega Major, which created a very striking-looking coach, though the Plaxton Panorama body was also made available, and one or two continental designs from builders such as Van Hool and Caetano were to appear on it in later years. Its small wheels gave a good ride for coach use, but also made a low

Above:
The YRT introduced underfloor engines to Bedford and it was used as both a service bus and a coach. A keen user of Bedfords as service buses was Maidstone Borough Transport; it used a variety of body builders though the Duple Dominant, shown here, was a common choice of service bus body on both Bedford and Ford.

floor available for buses, and a few operators took VAL buses, notably North Western which had a distinctive Strachans body built, specially contoured to fit under a low bridge. It remained in production until 1972.

The third model introduced in the 1960s was the VAM, a 33ft-long two-axle vehicle, suitable for 45-seat coach bodies but also used as a service bus by numerous operators, including major company operators which were not readily associated with light-weights. Among these were some of the nationalised Tilling undertakings, when no suitable Bristol model was available for their requirements, and the likes of Western National even had them with an ECW body similar to that built for the Bristol MW. It was introduced as the VAM5, with Bedford's 5.4litre 330 diesel, but later variants, like the VAL, were the VAM14 with the Leyland O.400 and the VAM70 with Bedford's 7.6litre 466.

Bedford was still the standard choice for light-weight vehicles, especially amongst the independent sector, though Ford was emerging as an increasingly strong competitor with its R192, which was very similar in concept and size to the VAM, and bigger R226.

The VAM was superseded in 1970 with the start of a new Bedford range. The YRQ used very similar components to the VAM, but arranged with the engine under the floor amidships. Hitherto the standard arrangement of underfloor engines was to use horizontal units, but Bedford managed to fit its 466 engine in vertically. Two years later the VAL was superseded by a 36ft version of the YRQ, the YRT, which had heavier components all round, shared with the 16-ton KM lorry range. Specification upgrades led to the largely similar YMQ and YMT, and a shortened version of the YMQ, the YMQS, was also made available.

There was something of a diversion from Bedford's mainstream production at the end of the 1970s. At the 1978 Motor Show it unveiled a highly-promising small bus, the JJL. This had a vertical 330 engine mounted transversely at the rear, driving though an Allison automatic gearbox and had a very stylish 27-seat body built by Marshall though developed in Bedford's own design studio. Unfortunately it never reached production; only four were built which saw service with a number of municipal operators, notably Maidstone and Brighton before being scattered amongst various independent operators. Unusually for such a rare type they achieved pretty well a full service life. Bedford's parent company foresaw little market for it and decided not to go into production. Given the runaway success of the Dennis Dart, a very similar design in many respects, it is possible that GM made the wrong decision, though perhaps the JJL was developed before its time had come. Another great British might-have-been . . .

During the 1980s the demands of coach operators were increasing; vehicles were required to work harder and run at high speeds over very high mileage, and the traditional lightweight began to be eclipsed by more sophisticated models, many from overseas. Bedford introduced turbocharging across the range in 1982, both to increase power outputs and to reduce emissions, and even the lowly NJM, as the SB had become, was available with turbocharging towards the end of its life — though in the same year as turbocharging was introduced Blue Coach Tours of St Helier, Jersey, was still buying 7ft 6in wide SBs with petrol engines. The YMT gave way to the

turbocharged YNT, which also boasted the six-speed ZF gearbox beloved of the heavyweights rather than the five-speed Turner with which Bedford had latterly been associated. However, Bedford was still lacking a 12m chassis (though specialist conversions of the YNTs were available), and this came in 1984 with the full 16tonne, air-sprung YNV, the first Bedford psv to gain a name, the Venturer. This had a 205bhp 8.2litre Blue Series turbocharged engine, still mounted vertically amidships, under the floor, and a ZF gearbox. It was a competent coach, with many heavyweight virtues yet still with a light weight and low cost, but fashion had dictated that Bedford was now a spent force, at least in the UK. The thousands of sales the company could record in a good year were down to a couple of hundred or so by the mid-1980s. Then General Motors tried to buy the struggling Leyland group from the Government during 1986 and was turned down on strategic grounds. The American group decided that Bedford was too small to survive in its own right, and closed it down. Thus production of Bedford buses and coaches ceased in 1986. The Bedford range passed to AWD, which never reintroduced psv chassis, and is now with Marshall of Cambridge, which has rights to use the Bedford name again. Given its involvement with buses again and its rôle in developing the JJL . . . well, you never know!

Bristol

The postwar history of Bristol Commercial Vehicles is an unusual one, in that of all manufacturers it was affected the most by the politics of the times. Like some other manufacturers, such as BMMO and AEC, its origins were in supplying vehicles to the operator which owned it, though its products quickly became

much more widespread than simply the Bristol Tramways Co, more often then not in conjunction with the bodybuilding subsidiary of another fellow Tilling group company, Eastern Counties, which later became a separate entity as Eastern Coach Works (ECW).

In 1937 it had launched a new range, the K double-decker and L single-decker, entirely conventional front-engined half-cab chassis with a Gardner 5LW engine and crash gearbox. Production of Ks restarted during the war, though with AEC engines, and postwar versions of both were offered in 1946, with a lowered radiator and bonnet line. Gardner 5LW, 6LW, AEC or Bristol's own AVW six-cylinder engines were available with four-speed or five-speed overdrive gearboxes. However, under the 1947 Transport Act various bus operators, including Bristol with its Motor Constructional Works, passed into state ownership, and Bristol was restricted to selling only within the state sector, though outstanding orders to other sectors could be completed. In some ways having a single, tied customer, tended to stifle development, and compared with the likes of Leyland and AEC Bristols tended to lack refinement and, in certain respects, engineering innovation. On the other hand their rugged simplicity, unstoppable reliability and excellent fuel consumption were denied to operators in other sectors who had learned to appreciate their charms.

The lack of technical innovation tended to be in the driveline department; Bristol drivers had to wrestle with crash gearboxes long after other manufacturers had made life easier. However, in other respects they were ahead of the field. The company operators of the nationalised Transport Holding Company tended to operate more in rural areas and as a such had a wide-

Above left:
A very promising Bedford design, which never got into full production, was the JJL, with a stylish Marshall-built body. They worked for a time at Brighton on the town centre shuttle service using an unusual livery in shades of orange.

Above:
A classic Bristol line-up at Eastern National's Braintree garage in 1971. Dual-purpose and bus versions of the MW flank an FLF-type Lodekka.
J. Rickard

Right:
A North Western Bristol L5G braves the snow in Buxton in February 1963.
A. Moyes

spread requirement for lowbridge double-deckers, with the awkward sunken gangway arrangement upstairs. Bristol was the first to address this problem, with its lowheight Lodekka. As introduced in 1949 twin prop shafts were used to take the drive to separate double-reduction differentials, using gears to bring the drive up from the low propshaft level to hub level and allowing thereby a dropped-centre axle. Production buses, which went into service from 1954, had a simpler arrangement with just one prop shaft. This new model, the LD, replaced the K-series, which had grown into the larger KS and wider KSW. Meanwhile the replacement for the L, which had like-

Top:
An early LD-type Bristol Lodekka of United at Bishop Auckland in 1959. Later LDs had a shorter radiator grille.
M. A. Sutcliffe

Above:
For rural use Bristol developed the diminutive SC4LK front-engined chassis. It was ideal for Crosville's operations in the more rural parts of North Wales, typified by this view of SSG606 near Henfryn in the Clwyd Valley in 1966.
A. Moyes

wise developed into the larger LL and LWL, was the LS, an underfloor-engined model offering a choice of Gardner 5HLW or 6HLW engines and a horizontal version of the Bristol unit, with integral bodywork by ECW, though some for the Scottish Bus Group were bodied by Alexander.

The LS was later replaced by the MW, with a separate chassis, though this dropped the Bristol engine option, while the very successful Lodekka was developed with a longer LDL version, and then from 1959 a new range with flat floors was introduced, the FS, with longer FL and forward-entrance FSF and FLF models. The Lodekka remained in production until

1968, by which time over 5,000 had been built. From 1956 onwards Dennis had been licensed to produce the Lodekka for outside customers as the Loline.

Bristol also built small numbers of smaller buses; the SC4LK was a small front-engined single-decker, in the mould of the Bedford SB and indeed using axles supplied by Bedford, though with a Gardner 4LK engine. This was replaced with a small underfloor-engined bus, the SU, which used a four-cylinder horizontal Albion engine.

Another innovation from Bristol in 1962 was the introduction of a single-deck chassis with the engine horizontally at the rear, the RE. This was available in two lengths and two frame heights, the high version giving space side luggage lockers for coach work. It was the first of a new wave of rear-engined single-deckers, and was also the most successful. The use of a front radiator helped improve weight distribution as well as cooling (indeed with several feet of piping and a cool-running Gardner engine cooling could be too good), while the engine was mounted closer to the rear axle than on other designs, with the Lodekka dropped-centre axle allowing a prop shaft to run over

Left:
The MW was the standard underfloor engined Bristol single-decker for the late 1950s/early 1960s. Scottish Omnibuses used this fleet of MW coaches to transport 1,000 wedding guests for Lord Bruce's wedding in Edinburgh; each carried a shield in Bruce tartan.

Above:
Seen leaving Basildon on the famous 151 Southend-London (Wood Green) service is a semi-automatic Bristol FLF6G of Eastern National.
W. T. Cansick

Left:
Bristol produced the most successful of the new-generation rear-engined single-deckers in the 1960s with its RE model. Seen in Wells in 1972 is a Bristol Omnibus one with the usual ECW bodywork in the reversed livery then used by Bristol for one-man operated services.
P. W. Robinson

Below left:
In 1965 Bristol products were once again available on the open-market. The first model sold to customers outside the THC was the RE, which was particularly popular with municipalities such as Colchester.
Kevin Lane

Above right:
Bristol introduced the lightweight underfloor-engined Bristol LH in 1968. It was available in various different lengths; the shortest was the LHS, which continued to be available primarily as a small coach chassis after the rest of the range was deleted. London Country had a few ECW-bodied LHSs.
Kevin Lane

Right:
National Bus Company standardised on the Bristol VRT for double-deck use. These two were in the PMT fleet; the one nearer the camera came from National Welsh.
Kevin Lane

the top of the axle to a gearbox mounted within the wheelbase. This arrangement put less strain on the vehicle's structure than other designs with all mechanical components in the rear overhang, and the remote mounting of the major components made for better heat dissipation. In true Bristol fashion a rather awkward manual gearbox was standard, though later the company was to bow to the inevitable and fit a semi-automatic unit, which improved the driver's lot no end.

Under THC ownership Bristol was set up as a separate manufacturing company, Bristol Commercial

Vehicles, in 1955. Then in 1965 Leyland took a 25% share in Bristol, allowing it to be opened up to other customers again, and the RE was made available with Leyland engines. It quickly sold to operators outside the nationalised sector.

Bristol was very late developing rear-engined double-deckers compared with Leyland and Daimler. Its first efforts appeared in 1966, unlike the other two using an in-line vertical engine in the rear offside corner. It was intended as a whole family of double- and single-deck vehicles, though after a couple of prototypes it was hurriedly re-engineered as the VRT, with the engine mounted transversely at the rear. The longitudinally-engined VRL remained on the stocks, but was specified only by one British operator, Ribble, with Leyland O.680 engines as a rather splendid 36ft motorway coach. Others were sold as buses to South Africa.

The National Bus Company was formed in 1969, and took over 50% of Bristol. Leyland increased its shareholding to become an equal partner with NBC, which adopted the VRT as its standard double-decker. Early versions were not up to Bristol's usual standard for reliability, but later Series 2 and Series 3 models improved things. somewhat. It clocked up sales of 4,474 before being superseded by the Leyland Olympian in 1982, though its success was largely due to National Bus Company. Again Gardner engines were standard, though later buses had the option of Leyland's 500-series fixed-head unit, and a few were built with Leyland O.680s when Gardners were difficult to come by.

At about the same time as the VRT was introduced Bristol announced a new single-decker, the lightweight LH. This was available in three lengths, the 9m LHS, 10m LH and 11m LHL, with mid-mounted Leyland 400 or Perkins engines. Now that the ban on outside sales was lifted it sold reasonably well as a coach to private-sector operators which might otherwise have bought Bedfords, though as a bus it

received support from the National Bus Company and London Transport in particular.

Leyland and National Bus Company set up a joint Bus Manufacturers Holdings company in 1975, which controlled Bristol, ECW and Leyland National, until NBC decided it was losing too much money and passed its shareholding to Leyland in 1982. Leyland had begun production of its Olympian at Bristol in 1981, ending VRT production at the same time. Meanwhile production of the RE continued for Northern Ireland and New Zealand, the last for Ulsterbus being built in 1982 despite the fact that home market customers had been refused REs since 1975, in favour of the Leyland National. Bristol built 4,629 REs.

Various factors conspired to depress the bus market during the 1980s; privatisation, deregulation and the phasing-out of bus grant all came about in the early years of the 1980s, and Leyland, anxious to cut surplus capacity, quickly decided to close Bristol, of which it had just gained control. Just over 1,000 Olympians were built there before the factory closed in September 1983.

Commer

Luton-based Commer was part of the Rootes Group, which took it over along with Humber in 1928. Its first postwar chassis was the Commando, which was in similar vein to the Bedford OB, though slightly bigger. It was in production from 1946 to 1949, during which time some 1,300 were built, with Commer's own four-litre petrol engine or the Perkins P6 diesel. It was popular for military use, especially with the Royal Air Force, though psvs were also built.

Below:
The Commer Commando was essentially a goods chassis, though could be bodied as a bus. This rather attractive vehicle was a Q3 with Cumberland 14-seat body for Watsons of Dundee.

Above:
An early Commer Avenger coach with the same style of front as fitted to contemporary Commer lorries. Built in 1949 it was one of a batch of four with Harrington 21-seat bodywork for Motorways (Overseas) of London SW1.

Right:
From 1954 Commer offered its new TS3 two-stroke diesel in the Avenger III. This early example has a Duple butterfly-fronted body of the type more readily associated with Bedford SB.

Below:
The Commer Avenger chassis, with the low-mounted TS3 diesel engine which avoided engine intrusion into the saloon.

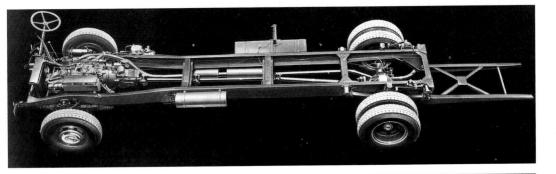

Quite a number had unusual one-and-a-half-deck observation-style bodywork, often for use by airlines for transfer work.

Commer was another manufacturer in the vanguard of underfloor-engined buses, though in a rather different vein from other manufacturers. Whereas the likes of AEC and Leyland were developing high-capacity single-deckers with the engine mounted amidships under the floor Commer was more interested in the coach market with the underfloor engine at the front, with a conventionally-positioned front axle. Here the aim was to rid the coach of engine intrusion. Like many manufacturers its new model was ready for the 1948 Commercial Motor Show; the Avenger was ahead of the pack of lightweight coach models in being forward control, thanks to the under-floor engine. The engine was Commer's own six-cylinder, 109bhp overhead valve unit. It was not a true horizontal unit, but the cylinders were set at 66° from vertical, a solution favoured much later by Ford and Scania as a way of minimising engine intrusion without going to the expense of developing a true horizontal unit. Many of the early Avenger Is featured the same frontal styling as Commer's contemporary truck range, which also used the underfloor engine.

The Avenger is not often considered a mainstream chassis, yet almost 1,000 Avenger Is were built before the larger Avenger II was introduced in response to the Bedford SB, which now took the lion's share of the market; thereafter Commer sales fell. Most of the sales were to small independents, though BOAC took sizeable numbers and many were exported.

In 1954 Commer offered its new TS3 diesel engine in the Avenger III. The TS3 is probably Commer's best-known achievement, though the engine had been developed by Tilling-Stevens which became part of the Rootes Group, of which Commer was a part, in 1953. The TS3 was a remarkable unit, a tiny, 3.26litre three-cylinder two stroke with supercharging and horizontally-opposed pistons, which despite its size was capable of producing 90bhp, and was later uprated to 105bhp. The sound effects were perhaps its most memorable feature! With its small dimensions and horizontal cylinders it was a natural for the Avenger, and was also supplied to Beadle and Harrington for their own integral designs (qv). However, the bus industry was never too adventurous with technology, and preferred more conventional engines with higher torque ratings, and the Avenger became an also-ran to the Bedford SB. Production of what had become the Avenger IV finished in 1964, by which time volumes had become very small indeed. Nonetheless sizeable batches were delivered to Southdown in particular, including 15 with Burlingham Seagull and 15 with Harrington body-work.

There were to be other Commer psvs, though; the 1500-series van was reasonably popular as a minibus in the 1960s — Crosville even took a pair in 1964 — and gained immortality as the archetypal postbus. It was rebadged Dodge (qv) in 1976 following the takeover of the Rootes Group by Chrysler three years earlier.

Crossley

It is perhaps a shame that Crossley Motors had a certain amount of difficulty translating its engineering innovation into production excellence. Crossley was well-known for its innovation, both in its bus and its car designs before the war. Unfortunately it was let down by a reputation for poor reliability and engine design.

The company had been based in Gorton in Manchester, though its factory was damaged during the war and postwar production began in a new factory at Errwood Park, just in Stockport. During the war it had developed a new double-decker, the DD42, and this was to be its mainstay model in the postwar years, along with a single-deck equivalent, the SD42. Crossley had been a major supplier to Manchester Corporation, which had evaluated the prototype DD42 in service. It was a largely conventional half-cab design, of which the most notable visual feature was a very low bonnet line, giving excellent visibility for the driver. Beneath the surface though was a new Crossley oil engine, the HOE7, which was to be the standard power unit for its postwar buses, whereas units such as the Gardner 5LW had also been available in prewar models, and it was coupled to a Brockhouse Turbo Transmitter torque-convertor transmission rather than a conventional gearbox.

Production buses turned out rather differently; constant mesh and later synchromesh gearboxes were considered in most cases a better bet than the unusual

Left:
Reading was quite a keen operator of Crossley DD42s; this one had lowbridge bodywork.

Below:
Disguising its Crossley origins well is this 1950 DD42 for Birmingham, with 'new look' front.

Right:
A CVE Omni owned by Kent County Council and operated by East Surrey around Edenbridge. Note the kneeling rear suspension to enable wheelchairs to be loaded at the rear.

Brockhouse unit, and whilst the prototype engine had acquitted itself very well last-minute redesign of the cylinder head was to strangulate the engine's air flow, leading to poor performance and a tendency to smoke. Crossley historian Mike Eyre attributes the head redesign to an reluctance to pay licence fees to Swiss manufacturer Saurer on whose patents the original head was designed. That reluctance may have led to the demise of the company. In 1948 it sold out to AEC, which bought Maudslay at the same time, to create ACV (Associated Commercial Vehicles).

Crossley DD42s tended to be a municipal bus; there were exceptions, but most turned up with municipal operators, more often than not with Crossley's own bodywork. The two biggest customers were Manchester, which had 301 postwar (plus the 1944 prototype) and Birmingham, which had 270, with its own style of bodywork. Birmingham's had the later downdraught version of the engine, with a revised cylinder head with more straightforward air intake arrangements, which overcame most of the earlier shortcomings of the engine. The last 100 delivered to Birmingham unusually had Birmingham's 'new look' front, with concealed radiator and wide bonnet.

However, Crossley's biggest triumph was a huge export order for Holland, to help re-equip the country's bus fleet after the war. Most of the 1,175 for Holland were SD42s with a supercharged, 150bhp version of the Crossley's engine, though 250 were tractor units to haul passenger semi-trailers.

When production ended of genuine Crossleys AEC built a small number of buses under the Crossley name, largely to gain extra stand space at Commercial Motor Shows but also to suit local pride; Darwen

Corporation for instance had a batch of Regent Vs with Crossley rather than AEC badges, showing Lancastrian solidarity (even if Crossley had ended its days just in Cheshire). The original Bridgemaster model was also developed at Crossley, which continued building bodywork until 1958, though it used AEC components and was later built at Park Royal on AEC subframes.

CVE/Omnicoach

City Vehicle Engineering set up production of an unusual minibus design from former railway engineering premises at Shildon, Darlington, in 1988. This was at the height of the 'minibus revolution', though when some of the shortcomings of van-based designs were becoming apparent. Its Omni was a licence-built version of an Austrian Steyr-Puch design, which used front-wheel drive in order to give a step-free entrance and low floor. Steyr's design was a halfcab, though CVE decided not to go back to that style once beloved of British builders, so its Omni had a slightly more conventional appearance than the Steyr — even if it was still a striking design. It was re-engineered for the British market with a Land Rover diesel engine, though others units became available such as a Perkins Phaser.

Its low-floor credentials meant it sold rather better to the welfare sector than it did to psv operators, though a few are in service in the psv sector for specialist applications. CVE went out of business in 1990, but the Omni is still built by Omnicoach, set up the following year to continue the design. It now uses a Mazda turbocharged diesel engine. A longer, three-axle version has also been developed.

Daimler

Daimler boasted a fine reputation for the refinement and quality of its cars, and this extended to its buses. Early on it had taken to using fluid transmission, with a preselector gearbox, which not only made life easier for the driver, it gave rise to one of the most characteristic features of Daimler's vehicles, a delightfully melodious transmission. Daimler also used very effective flexible engine mounts to give its buses a smoothness which few could match.

Based in Coventry, Daimler restarted bus production in Wolverhampton during the war and afterwards introduced its Coventry-built Victory series, better known by its type designation which changed according to the engine specified. Daimler offered a choice of engines; its own CD6 in the CVD6, AEC in the CVA6 and Gardner 5LW or 6LW in the CVG5 and CVG6. Another Daimler characteristic on all its vehicles, buses included, was the fluted radiator top. The CV was available as a single-decker or double-decker, and in single-deck form was popular for coach use. Many major municipalities took Daimlers, the most common variant being the CVG6, and Birmingham specified its 'new look' concealed radiator from 1950, later adopted as standard by Daimler. The last traditional exposed radiator chassis was built in 1953, and the fluted radiator top disappeared, though a stylised version adorned the grille of some of the 'new look' examples. Manchester then specified a narrower bonnet with the headlights separate in 1957, and this too was adopted as standard.

At around the same time 30ft models became available, with semi-automatic transmission as an option to preselective, and a David Brown synchromesh gearbox was also offered, the designation, with Gardner 6LW engine, becoming CSG6.

Daimler was sold by its BSA parent to Jaguar in 1960, and the following year Jaguar also took over Guy, whose constant-mesh gearbox replaced the David Brown unit in manual gearbox versions, as CCG5 or CCG6. Home production ended in 1968, although 34ft long versions were built for Hong Kong until 1971. Some 11,000 had been built.

An interesting diversion was the CD650 introduced in 1948. This was a rather more sophisticated beast altogether, with power-hydraulic systems for the brakes, preselector gearbox and to give power steering. Power was provided in abundance by a new 10.5-litre (650cu in) Daimler engine, for which a wider version of Daimler's standard radiator was supplied, giving an impressive appearance for an impressive bus. The notoriously conservative British bus industry did not take to it; only a few were built, mainly for Derbyshire independent Blue Bus and Halifax Corporation. However, it did sell slightly better as an export single-decker.

The same engine was used in horizontal form in Daimler's next single-deck design, the Freeline, which began life in 1951. It used a five-speed preselective gearbox, and there was an option of Gardner 6HLW engine. Again it was much more successful as an export chassis than a home-market one, though around 70 were built as coaches for UK use, with another 20

Left:
Salford City Transport took a large batch of MCW-bodied Daimler CVG6s in 1951, and needed no more new buses for about 10 years. They had an unusual short version of the standard Daimler exposed radiator. Also unusual is 437's reversed livery.
M. A. Sutcliffe

Above:
Manchester was also a keen Daimler user; for most of the 1950s and 1960s it dual-sourced between Leyland and Daimler. In 1954/55 it took 70 rather elegant MCW-bodied CVG6s, of which two are seen in Piccadilly when new.

Left:
With the later style of front is Huddersfield 431, a 1964 Roe-bodied CVG6LX-30, a type bought by Huddersfield for trolleybus replacement. It is seen in Bradford soon after the formation of West Yorkshire PTE; although the Daimler shows no evidence of PTE ownership the Bradford AEC Regent and Daimler Fleetline behind carry the PTE's new livery. *Kevin Lane*

Below left:
Sunderland used a distinctive style of Roe bodywork on a batch of nine Daimler Fleetlines in 1963. *M. A. Sutcliffe*

Top left:
Alexander brought a new style to rear-engined double-deckers in the early-1960s, as shown on this 1965 Fleetline of North Western, seen at Lower Mosley Street bus station, Manchester.

Top right:
The Fleetline was intended for double-deck use, but a single-deck version was also made available. This rather neat Roe-bodied bus was new to Halifax in 1967. *L. J. Wright*

Above:
West Midlands PTE standardised on Daimler Fleetlines, a type chosen by most of its constituent operators. An MCW-bodied Fleetline picks up in central Birmingham. *Kevin Lane*

Right:
Daimler's purpose-built rear-engined single-deck chassis was the Roadliner, which looked highly impressive when bodied by Marshall for PMT, the biggest UK user of the type. Reliability was sadly less impressive.

or so buses. However, well over 500 were exported.

Daimler turned its attentions to rear-engined chassis in the 1960s. The first was the Fleetline, a transverse rear-engined double-decker introduced in 1960. This broadly resembled Leyland's Atlantean, which went into production two years earlier, though with the important difference that a dropped-centre rear axle was used to give an overall low height. An ingenious semi-automatic gearbox was developed for it, in which the drive passed back through the gearbox through a hollow shaft running through the centre of the gearbox, to give a compact driveline. Daimler engines were to be offered, but the more popular Gardner 6LX became the standard unit, with the 6LXB offered from 1969.

Rather less successful was the single-deck Roadliner. This 36ft rear-engined chassis began with a horizontal Daimler CD6 unit, unusually mounted transversely, using otherwise the same driveline as the Fleetline. However, production buses used a simpler, in-line driveline and straight rear axle, with a Cummins V6 engine chosen for its compact dimensions. However, this proved a highly unsuccessful unit in this application, and a later move to a Perkins V8 did little to improve the model's fortunes, neither did a last-ditch attempt to fit the AEC-built Leyland 800-series 13.1litre V8. It had air or rubber suspension, and made an impressive coach chassis, with a

power output of 192bhp from its fast-revving Cummins, and had the virtue of a low, step-free entrance for bus use. Fewer than 200 were built for the UK market, and a single-deck version of the Fleetline proved rather more popular.

The Fleetline was altogether a very popular chassis, and unlike previous Daimler models sold strongly to company operators as well as municipalities, helped by the lack of a rear-engined double-decker from AEC. London Transport also standardised on the Fleetline for rear-engined deliveries, and its inability to adapt to rear-engined types brought something of a smear to the Fleetline's reputation.

Jaguar had merged with the British Motor Corporation (BMC) in December 1966, to form British Motor Holdings (BMH), which merged again with Leyland in May 1968 to form British Leyland, thereby bringing Daimler and Guy into common ownership with Leyland, AEC and Bristol. As a result Leyland O.680 engines became available in the Fleetline from 1970. However, in 1973 Leyland decided to move Fleetline production from Coventry to its own factory, after 7,224 Daimler Fleetlines had been built. Another 1,500 Daimler Fleetlines were built by Leyland, before the name was changed to the Leyland Fleetline at the end of 1974. Production continued until 1980, by which time almost 11,750 Fleetlines had been built.

Dennis

For the first 90 or so years of its 100-year history Dennis, based in Guildford, Surrey, was really one of the 'also-rans' of the bus industry. It was never an insignificant manufacturer — but then it wasn't all that significant either! At one time it produced so many short runs of odd models that it was considered that anything suggesting a production line was frowned upon at Guildford. That may be an overstatement of the case, but Dennis always made a great play of being flexible in its offering.

For a period it even came out of bus manufacture altogether; few buses were built after 1965 and bus production ground to a halt for 10 years from 1967. What is remarkable indeed is the fact that Dennis is not only one of the most significant players in the British bus market in the 1990s it is now the only British-owned chassis manufacturer, having outlasted many much more significant bus manufacturers, not least the mighty Leyland and AEC.

Dennis's main postwar models were the Lance double-decker and Lancet single-decker, basically conventional half-cab types with front engines and manual gearboxes, though with a preselective overdrive on the Lancet. There was a choice of Gardner or Dennis's own 7.6litre O.6 engine. The Lance K2 had the Gardner engine, while the K3 had Dennis's engine and the K4, built for Dennis's local operator Aldershot & District from 1954, had the Gardner 5LW and 'new-look' front.

While other manufacturers used identical bonnets and radiators on both single and double-deck models

Below:
A 30ft long Dennis Lancet III with full-front Gurney Nutting 39-seat bodywork of Major's Coaches, Worksop.

the Lance and Lancet had quite different styles. Most Lancets were built as coaches for independent operators, but Aldershot & District, Yorkshire Traction, East Kent and Merthyr Tydfil were other major operators of the original postwar J3 type, which was also available in full-front form as the J3A. The later 30ft version was the J10 series.

Unusually for a manufacturer of heavyweight conventional chassis Dennis also offered a lighter-weight, normal-control bus, the Falcon, with a choice of Dennis petrol or diesel engines or the Gardner 4LK. Again larger operators included East Kent and Aldershot & District. A full-front forward-control version was also built in small numbers.

Dennis joined the underfloor-engine bandwagon in 1950, with its sophisticated Dominant model, which featured a horizontal version of the O.6 engine, available with a turbocharger and Hobbs automatic transmission. However, Dennis introduced a rather simpler — and lighter — underfloor-engined Lancet in 1952, and this proved rather more successful in both coach and bus forms. Following the trend to yet lighter weight, as demonstrated by the Leyland Tiger Cub and AEC Reliance, Dennis introduced the lightweight Pelican in 1956, which used some Falcon components, including a horizontal version of the five-litre Dennis engine. Only one was completed, but gave good service.

Rather more successful than other Dennis postwar designs was the Loline double-decker, which was a licence-built version of the Bristol Lodekka. It was first shown at the 1956 Commercial Motor Show, in 30ft form; nearly all Lolines were to this length. It was available with a variety of engines, including Gardner 6LW, 6LX, Leyland O.600 and AEC AV470. A forward-entrance Loline II came in 1958, and as the F-series Lodekka included various improvements such as a flatter floor and improved frontal appearance, similar improvements to the

Dennis resulted in the Loline III in 1960 — though the new version had more Dennis content than the earlier models. Most Loline IIIs were 30ft long and forward entrance, coinciding with FLF version of the Lodekka, though the first two, for Leigh, had rear-entrance bodywork. The last were built for Halifax in 1967, with semi-automatic transmission, and Dennis then withdrew from the psv market, though a pair of Pax V lorry chassis were bodied by Dennis as buses for Llandudno later that year.

Dennis had come into the ownership of the Hestair Group in 1971. By the mid-1970s some operators were concerned at the monopoly being built up by Leyland at the time, and Dennis was persuaded to re-

enter the market. It developed a new rear-engined double-deck chassis, with a Gardner 6LXB engine mounted transversely, driving through a Voith auto-matic gearbox. In order to test the driveline a former Leeds Corporation Daimler CVG6 was fitted with a 6LXB engine and Voith transmission and ran in service with a number of operators, including London Transport, and Leicester City Transport, which came to be something of a champion of Dennis's new range as it developed.

Once the double-decker, named the Dominator, was launched a single-deck version followed. Both sold steadily, mainly to the municipal sector, though the breakthrough came when South Yorkshire

Above:
Aldershot & District was again a major customer for the normal-control Dennis Falcon; indeed it was the only customer for this P5 model, of which it had 23 with Strachans 30-seat bodywork. 248 (LOU 76) was built in 1954 and had a Gardner 4LK engine.

Left:
The Loline was a licence-built version of the Bristol Lodekka made available for operators outside the state sector. This Loline I was operated by Middlesbrough Corporation and had Northern Counties rear-entrance bodywork.
M. A. Sutcliffe

Right:
The last customer for the Loline was Halifax, which took a batch of Loline IIIs with Gardner 6LX engines, semi-automatic transmission and Northern Counties bodywork in 1967.

Above:
The first Dennis model when it restarted bus production in 1977 was the Dominator. National Bus Company tried five with Willowbrook bodywork with Maidstone & District, whose Medway Towns routes had some formidable hills and sizeable loadings and were thus ideal for testing new bus types. 5302 is seen at Walderslade in 1980.

Right:
The Dominator was also available as a single-decker, often with the distinctively-styled Marshall Camair 80 body. Looking very smart having just been acquired from Merthyr Tydfil in 1985 was Chester 113 (CKG 215V).
Roy Marshall

Transport adopted the Dominator as its standard bus, normally with Alexander bodywork. South Yorkshire had become a keen user of Voith transmission, which suited its hilly terrain, though it specified the Rolls-Royce Eagle engine in place of the Gardner. It built up a fleet of 450. The Dominator remains nominally on the market at the time of writing, though in practice few have been built in recent years. However, it has spawned three-axle versions, the Condor and Dragon, which are selling well in the Far East. It now features the Cummins L10 engine as standard, and air suspension, introduced as an option to the standard leaf springs, is now also standard.

In 1980 a purpose-built single-deck chassis was developed from the Dominator. This was the Falcon, with a Gardner 6HLXB mounted horizontally behind the rear axle. Other versions were available, notably the Falcon V, with Mercedes-Benz or Perkins V8 engines, the former suitable for double-deck use, the latter developed in conjunction with National Express for high-speed long-distance coach use. Neither helped Dennis's efforts to re-establish itself; the National Express vehicles in particular soon showed up their rapid development in frequent, high-profile failures. If the Dominator was a reborn Daimler Fleetline, the Falcon V was a latter-day Roadliner.

While Dennis had been out of the bus market, it had continued to produce lorries, fire engines and refuse vehicles, and the next bus model was built on the same production line as these. This was the

Top left:
In the days before the purpose-built Dart was available
Dennis built a midibus version of the Dominator, the
Domino, for Greater Manchester and South Yorkshire
PTEs. They had Perkins engines and Maxwell trans-
mission, and the Greater Manchester ones had smart
Northern Counties bodywork. They replaced Seddons
on the Centreline service in Manchester.

Above left:
The South Yorkshire Dominos were the first vehicles
bodied by the fledgling Optare. Though a competent
body, Optare had yet to find its feet on the styling front.
Kevin Lane

Top:
As Dennis branched out into underfloor engined
designs it came up with a full heavyweight, offering the
Gardner 6HLXCT engine and Voith transmission, the
Dorchester. Though intended as a coach, Geoff Amos
of Daventry had some with rather functional, high-
capacity Reeve Burgess bodywork for schools use.
Kevin Lane

Above:
The rear-engined Falcon was a promising design,
offering an in-line engine and straight driveline. Most
popular was the HC version, with the Gardner 6HLXB
engine, though East Lancs contrived to come up with
some less than inspired body designs for it. This one is
Chesterfield 43 (TWJ 343Y).
Kevin Lane

The Falcon V had a vertical vee-formation engine of either Perkins or Mercedes-Benz manufacture. After coach deregulation Dennis built 11 for National Express with high-floor Duple Goldliner bodywork; National Express wanted a British-built vehicle able to compete on equal terms with the foreign competition. Unfortunately it wanted them in a hurry, and inadequate time for testing showed itself in woeful unreliability; it was a shame, as they performed superbly and could compete with the best for ride quality, comfort and noise levels. They should have been a major boost to Dennis's credibility, but had the reverse effect; Dennis had to make up much ground to get to the position it now enjoys.

Lancet — by now Dennis was keen on reusing old names. The Lancet was a lightweight mid-engined chassis, using Perkins vertical engines, either the straight-six 6.354 or the V8 540. It sold modestly as a bus, and was also offered in short-wheelbase form, in which version it sold reasonably well as a coach with Van Hool bodywork, often called the Lancette.

The Lancet was also developed into a Gardner-engined heavyweight, known as the Dorchester, which sold reasonably well to the Scottish Bus Group, but had only a few other takers.

The Lancette had shown there was a market for a medium-weight coach and in 1987 Dennis took a new approach with the Javelin. There was much less flexibility of specification than with traditional Dennises;

Left:
Perhaps the greatest white elephant of Dennis's return to the bus market was the Mercedes-powered double-deck version of the Falcon V. However Greater Manchester's pair, with Northern Counties bodywork, were still in service 10 years after they were built. Dennis's East Lancs-bodied demonstrator ended up as a playbus in Stevenage when only two years old; when the author drove it the sound effects reminded him of a Flying Fortress!
John Robinson

it had a vertical Cummins C-series engine and a ZF gearbox mounted immediately ahead of the rear axle, an arrangement which allowed space for luggage within the wheelbase, like a rear-engined chassis, but with a rear boot too. The Javelin went into full production in 1988, and benefited from Bedford's demise; it quickly became the successor to Bedford in the coach market and gave Dennis its real breakthrough.

Dennis had suddenly become rather good at spotting niches in the market, and the rear-engined Dart was to be its greatest triumph yet. While minibuses had become the norm, nobody had ventured into producing a small, simple bus chassis with a rear engine. The Dart was a narrow-track vehicle, available in 8.5m, 9m and 9.8m lengths with a Cummins B-series in-line engine at the rear and Allison transmission. Large orders were won in London, and many other operators were attracted by it, such that 2,000 were built in four years.

In 1992 a new full-size single-decker came in, the Lance, with an in-line Cummins C-series engine at the rear. This has since been developed into the SLF low-floor bus, the first British-built offering in this market. It is also understood that a double-deck version is to be launched during 1995, though the Dominator will remain on the market.

Dennis became part of the Trinity Holdings group in January 1989, following a management buyout from Hestair.

Above:
Dennis had rather more success with the lighter-weight mid-engined Cummins-powered Javelin, which was suitable for both bus and coach use. One bus user was Eastern Counties, which had a batch of 10 with Plaxton Derwent II bodywork in 1990.
Kevin Lane

Right:
Dennis's major success of the 1990s has been the Dart, seen here in its original form with Carlyle bodywork.

Above:
The most popular body for the Dart is Plaxton's Pointer, now the standard for Badgerline group companies amongst others. Two are seen with Badgerline subsidiary South Wales Transport in Swansea.

Left:
Dennis's current full-sized rear-engined single-deck range is rather more successful than the Falcon. London Buses was the first customer for its Lance, which has a vertical in-line Cummins C-series engine at the rear and a delightfully simple construction. London's first ones were for Selkent, replacing Routemasters on the 36B, and have attractive Alexander bodywork.

Below left:
The Lance is proving a versatile design; the first variation on the theme was the SLF low-floor chassis, which East Kent uses on the Canterbury Park-&-Ride service with Berkhof bodywork.

Dodge/Renault

Dodge has had a number of incarnations and allegiances down the years. It is a well-known American name, but in Britain has a more chequered history, latterly tied up more with French manufacturers than American. It also became part of the Rootes Group, itself taken over by Chrysler, and while much of the former Rootes Group finished up in French hands as Peugeot Talbot the British Dodge finished up in the hands of Peugeot's great French rival, Renault, whose name superseded Dodge before the Dunstable factory was closed down.

It offered its first true psv chassis from its Kew factory in 1962. It was a lightweight, aimed at the market dominated by Bedford and Ford, though it had the advantage over the other two of offering a true front entrance on a 31ft chassis; at this stage Bedford only offered this feature on its 36ft three-axle VAL. The S306 had a front-mounted Leyland O.370 engine, while the S307 used a Perkins 6.354. It sold only in small numbers; the most significant order was for six S307s with Strachans bodywork for London coach operator Rickards. It was withdrawn from the market in 1967.

Chrysler took an interest in the Rootes Group in 1964, and gained control in 1973. Three years later the Commer range was rebadged as Dodge. By this time the only Commer psv was a minibus, on which the Post Office had standardised for the Postbus services. It also used the same vehicle as its standard van for telephones in the days before British Telecom had been invented. In bus form it was known as the PB1500, and it was as late as 1984 that the last of these entered service, despite the design dating back to the early 1960s and being considered decidedly obsolete in any other market.

Dodge also gained a range of larger vans and trucks from Commer, and these too were available as minibuses and buses. What had begun life as the Commer Walkthru van had developed into a chassis cab, and sold in small numbers as a minibus, later becoming the Dodge 50-series. At one time it was also sold as a Karrier, though bearing little resemblance to traditional Huddersfield-built Karriers of prewar years!

Small numbers, that was, until the second wave of minibus mania struck after deregulation. This followed the realisation that the 16-seater, represented primarily by the Ford Transit and Freight Rover Sherpa, had quickly been outgrown by the volume of traffic. At first there was a little gap in the market for larger minibuses; Mercedes was revamping its range and there was little other choice until the Metrorider and Optare CityPacer came on stream, and the Dodge 50, in S46 and larger S56 variants, suddenly became popular as the rather basic chassis for a minibus. At one stage demand for 50s was so high that supplies of the optional Chrysler Torqueflite automatic gearbox were being air-freighted from the USA to keep up with demand. The chassis was especially popular amongst the local-authority sector, where political pressures meant that foreign-built vehicles were not considered to be quite the thing. Greater Manchester Buses for one took to the type in very big numbers, with Northern Counties bodywork, but other PTCs such as West Midlands Travel and South Yorkshire Transport also took to it, as did some of the former municipal operators such as Ipswich, Chester, Cleveland Transit and Eastbourne, and the Scottish Bus Group. In 1990 London Buses also bought 123 of the larger S75 which had been made available for psv operators wanting vehicles up to 33 seats, though many of the London ones have since been sold prematurely. By this time Renault had taken over Dodge and replaced the name with Renault; ironically

Right:
A rather basic Dodge S300-series. It was originally a demonstrator and was bodied by Mulliner.
Stewart J. Brown

those operators which were keen not to be seen to be buying foreign chassis found themselves buying Renaults!

Other vehicles from the Commer range were the Commando G08 and larger G10, with front Perkins engines. Most were built on virtually unmodified truck chassis, with the axle at the front, and became popular with the military and British Airways for crew transfer work, mainly with Wadham Stringer bodywork. However, the chassis were made available with a set-back front axle, allowing a proper front entrance. In reality the chassis was still virtually unmodified, with just an extension ahead of the front axle, and even the driver's position remained the same giving an odd sensation of driving from what seemed like halfway down the bus! The most celebrated was a small GO8 built for Strathclyde PTE for use on Arran, with a demountable body. Thus it could be used as a bus morning and evening and swap its body for a van to deliver goods during the day. The idea did not catch on, and neither did the Dodge Commando.

Renault ended production at Dunstable in March 1993 and the range has now come to an end.

Douglas

Better known for logging and cross-country vehicles Douglas Equipment of Cheltenham launched a straight-framed, front-engined single-decker with Meadows four-cylinder engine and gearbox during the 1950s. The design was intended for both home market and export.

Duple

Above:
The impressive Duple Integral 425 coach.

After the War Britain had a considerable number of bus and coach bodybuilders; best known of the latter was Hendon-based Duple, which became known throughout the country for its coach bodies on Bedford chassis, though built on other chassis in smaller numbers too. In 1960 it took over Burlingham of Blackpool and progressively moved production there, until it closed down in Hendon in 1968. In 1965 Harringtons closed down, and thereafter Plaxton and Duple were the 'big two' in British coach building, both solidly traditional and continuing to build separate bodies on others' chassis.

However, after the 1980 Transport Act liberalised coaching there was a sudden move by British coach operators towards the exotic coaches built on the Continent, including rear-engined integrals. Thus Duple began to look towards producing its own integrals, and built a single Caribbean body on a Neoplan underframe. This was not to lead very far, but for the 1984 and 1985 seasons Duple entered an agreement with Bova, the Dutch integral manufacturer, to build a special, low-height version of the Caribbean on a Bova Europa frame, which in turn was based on DAF running units. This emerged as the Duple Calypso, which enjoyed a reasonable following.

Though the Calypso never achieved huge volumes the experience was useful in the development of Duple's own full integral, the very striking and impressive Integral 425, which was announced at the 1984 Motor Show. In 1983 Duple had become part of the Hestair Group, owner of Dennis, and some Dennis expertise went into the underframe of the new Duple. It featured a rear-mounted Cummins L10 engine, though DAF was later offered as an option, driving through ZF manual or automatic transmission.

The 425 had a number of innovative features. The driving position was placed at the very front of the vehicle, close up to the nearly vertical windscreen, over which was a distinctive raked-back glass panel, strongly tinted in an attempt to prevent the driver frying in the summer. The forward mounting of the driver was combined with a special seat design in order to maximise capacity; the Duple 425 was able to seat 61 passengers, a record for a 12m single-deck coach, though fortunately most operators took pity on their passengers and used the capacity to give 57 seats at a pitch usually found in a 53-seater. A special stainless-steel frame was developed for it, and the external styling was not only impressive but was aerodynamically efficient too; the 425 designation represented its low drag coefficient. At that time coefficient of drag had suddenly become all the rage following Ford's recently introduced Sierra and Audi's 80 and 100 car ranges, whose unusual styling was justified by their low coefficient of drag; Audi even displayed a cd figure on their cars. In Duple's case the combination of good aerodynamics and the very efficient Cummins L10 engine led to excellent fuel consumption, often in the order of 12mpg or more, comparing with a coach industry standard of about 10mpg. Given its high carrying capacity it was thus a very economical proposition and it sold reasonably well.

Hestair decided to close down Duple in 1990, in the face of dwindling orders for both buses and coaches, and sold the coach designs to arch-rival Plaxton. Plaxton decided to keep the 425 going, and built it in France at the factory of French coachbuilder Lorraine, which Plaxton had taken over, though with finishing work undertaken at its Scarborough factory. It only built the design for one season however.

Foden

Fodens Ltd, based in Sandbach, Cheshire, was well-known as a high-quality heavyweight lorry manufacturer, and remains in business as such, though now in the American ownership of Paccar. However, it did also build some buses, on a comparatively small scale, and these, like the lorries, were manufactured to a high standard and embodied much innovation and refinement.

Foden's first bus had been built for its famous works band in 1933, and another 10 buses and coaches were built up to 1935. However, it restarted bus production in 1945 with a PVD6 double-deck demonstrator. The most immediately 'different' feature of the Foden was its full-width bonnet and concealed radiator, well ahead of the later fashion for such things, though there was much more innovation under the surface, such as hydraulic brakes and an unusual cab design, with the speedometer in the middle of the steering wheel. That first PVD6 had a Gardner 6LW engine, the standard unit in its double-deck output, and a Foden constant-mesh four-speed gearbox. It was followed the next year with a single-decker, the PVSC6, with a five-cylinder PVSC5 version. Most single-deck Fodens were built as

coaches, some using the tidy frontal treatment to produce a very effective full-front design. The excellent ride quality and attention to details such as engine mounting made it especially suitable for coach use.

At the 1948 Commercial Motor Show Foden unveiled its own two-stroke engine, the FD6. This was a 4.1-litre unit with a Rootes supercharger giving 126bhp at 2,000rpm, and had made its debut in what was nominally a PVSC6 coach in 1947. A similar engine was fitted in a double-deck demonstrator in that year, which later passed to Warrington, the largest operator of Foden double-deckers. It remained unique as a double-decker, though the two-stroke did appear in 53 single-deckers, which were designated PVFE6 when so fitted.

In 1950 Foden introduced a rather more revolutionary chassis. This was a single-deck coach chassis which moved to the style of the day with full-front bodywork with setback front axle, though instead of going to an underfloor engine Foden adopted a transverse rear-engine position, again offering the choice

of Foden's two-stroke engine (PVRF6) or the Gardner 6LW, though retaining the constant-mesh gearbox. A Foden-engined chassis appeared at the Festival of Britain in 1951 before being exported to Spain and bodied by Ayats. The rear-engined Fodens were not a great success, although 54 were built for the home market by the time production ended in 1954, a surprising number of them with Foden engines, and several more were exported. The last did not enter service until 1958, with Toppings, Liverpool, having been used as an experimental chassis by Fodens.

Top:
Foden chassis often carried rather exotic coach body-work; Salopia of Whitchurch, Shropshire, had a number of Fodens; this 1950 two-stroke PVFE6 had splendid observation bodywork by Whitson, with stylish faired-in rear wheels.

Above:
Smiths Imperial of Birmingham built its own bodywork on this 1949 PVFE6; the distinctive frontal styling disguises what was otherwise quite a conservative style.

Top:
A number of Fodens had Crellin Duplex-style half-deck bodywork; this one for the Dutch airline KLM was built by Lincolnshire Trailers in 1951. It was possible to cram anything up to 52 seats in such bodywork.

Above:
Whitson managed a classically understated style of bodywork for this Foden PVRF6, built for Nottinghamshire-based Netherfield Coaches in 1951.

Left:
This Foden PVRF6 was exhibited on Associated Coach Builders' stand at the 1952 Earls Court show.

Bodywork was usually by Whitson, Gurney Nutting,
Bellhouse Hartwell or Plaxtons, and Lawton — a
bodybuilder generally associated with Foden — also
offered a bus body. In the event though all but one of
the home-market ones were bodied as coaches.

Meanwhile conventional Foden production
continued, the last being five PVD6 double-deckers
with East Lancs bodywork for Warrington in
1955/56. Some 450 chassis had been built in 10 years,
including about 75 exports, mostly to Australia.

That was not quite the end of the story however.
Leyland's decision to drop the Fleetline in the mid-
1970s meant the end of any Gardner-engined double-
decker on the market, prompting one or two other
manufacturers to have a go at this gap in the market.
Foden developed a semi-integral rear-engined double-
deck chassis with transverse Gardner 6LXB engine
and Allison transmission, which was launched in
1978. It was built in conjunction with Northern
Counties as the Foden-NC, and two were built for
Greater Manchester PTE. One-off Northern Counties-
bodied vehicles were built for West Yorkshire PTE,
West Midlands PTE, Derby City Transport and PMT,
which evaluated the design against a Bristol VRT and
a Dennis Dominator on behalf of National Bus
Company. Another was bodied by East Lancs for
South Yorkshire and the last chassis was never
bodied. Foden decided not to proceed with the
project.

Ford/Thames

Ford Motor Co is so well-known throughout automotive circles that it is surprising how recent a
newcomer it is as a builder of psvs. It was in June
1957 that it first announced its intention to enter the
market — although there had been Ford-based psvs
before, not least on Model Ts in the early days of
motorbuses, especially in rural areas.

Traditionally Ford had used other names for its
commercial vehicles, such as Fordson or Thames, and
the new entrant, based on the Thames Trader lorry
range, was marketed as a Thames. It was a seven-ton
chassis, almost identical in concept to the Bedford SB
with which it competed head-on. Indeed with identical body styles it took a keen eye to tell a Thames
from an SB. The front-mounted engine, over the front
axle, just like an SB, was a new Ford 5.4-litre unit
developing 100bhp at 2,500rpm driving through a
four-speed synchromesh gearbox, and brakes were
servo-assisted hydraulic. There was also an option of
a 4.9litre petrol engine.

The Thames was an instant success, leaping into
second place behind the Bedford SB in its particular
market segment, with nearly 500 sold in the first year.
Although Fords were very much in the lightweight
sector the manufacturer was keen to stress the forti-
tude of the design, and a prototype ran from London
to Moscow and back, in under 45 hours, and down the
years Fords went on a number of mammoth journeys,
ostensibly for proving but doubtless more for
publicity.

Ford stole something of a march on Bedford in
1963, when it introduced a 36ft two-axle chassis;
Bedford of course had gone down the unconventional

three-axle road for its 36ft VAL. The new chassis was the Thames 36; it used the same engine as the shorter chassis, now named Thames 30, though with a five-speed gearbox and air brakes. The engine remained at the front, though now ahead of the front axle. However, it was somewhat underpowered and was replaced in 1965 by the much more successful R-series. This increased the power output up to a maximum of 150bhp by introducing turbocharging, rather a rare thing to do, especially in a lightweight chassis, at this time.

Two versions were available, the R192, a direct competitor for the Bedford VAM, and the R226, a direct replacement for the Thames 36. Both designations implied the wheelbase in inches, and were metricated as the R1014 and R1114 respectively in 1971. The Thames name was also dropped, and the new chassis proved much more successful. They now

Above:
Ford's first 36ft coach was the Thames 36; unlike Bedford's VAL Ford was able to build to the new maximum length on two axles. This prototype, seen in France on a proving run, carried Duple Marauder bodywork.

Left:
Ford's R-series was popular amongst independent operators for bus use as well as coach use; bus grant enabled them to buy new lightweight service buses very cheaply. This Willowbrook-bodied R1014 was operated by Osbornes of Tollesbury.
Kevin Lane

became a close second to Bedford in the market
place, rather than trailing behind, the turbocharged
engines giving a livelier performance than the
contemporary Bedfords.

Surprisingly the National Bus Company was to
become a major customer for the Ford R-series, and
there was a vogue for them to replace heavyweights,
even turning up in fleets like Southdown for long-
distance work previously the preserve of heavyweights like the Leyland Leopard, while operators
such as United Counties and South Wales used them
for service bus work. Scottish Bus Group was an even
more enthusiastic user, with bus and dual-purpose
version of the Alexander Y-type body and Duple
Dominant coach bodywork too.

The manual gearbox was something of a hindrance
for bus work, and in 1974 Ford announced an innovative, semi-automatic control for its six-speed synchromesh gearbox. This was electronically controlled and
although manufacturers such as Scania and Volvo

were to adopted similar solutions a decade or so later
it never went into production at this stage. However,
Ford announced an Allison automatic option for the
R-series in 1976 which increased its appeal for bus
work.

The chassis was modified in 1977 by inclining the
engine 45° to the nearside, to provide a better
entrance and to reduce intrusion and noise, while six-
speed gearboxes were offered. At the same time the
Turbo II engine was fitted, a six-litre 141bhp unit
from the contemporary D-series lorry, and a modified
radiator was fitted allowing the chassis to take the
Duple Dominant II body for the first time.

The last version was the R1015/R1115 with
improved Dover engines, which came from the new

Above:
Later the Ford Transit was to become familiar nation-wide on local bus services. The revolution can be said to have started in Exeter, with Devon General; this is one of many hundreds bodied by Carlyle for National Bus Company.

Cargo range replacing the D-Series lorries. Still a six-litre unit, power was now up to 153bhp, and gross vehicle weight was increased to 12.6tonnes on the R1115. However, like Bedford Ford was feeling the cold from the new wave of coaching, requiring much harder work from vehicles and higher standards for passengers, which favoured heavyweights. Production slumped during the 1980s and finally ended in 1985, when Ford announced it would not build a successor to the R-series. This left the lightweight sector to Bedford, to which Ford had always been No 2, but Bedford was not to stay the course much longer either.

In 1973 Ford announced a new medium-sized chassis, the A-series. This fitted into its commercial vehicle range between the D-series and the Transit. In appearance it was like a big version of the Transit, with a short bonnet and was designed for gross vehicle weights from 3.5 to 6.5 tons. It offered a choice of two-litre V4 and three-litre V6 petrol or four-cylinder 2.4litre or six-cylinder 3.6litre diesel engines and four or five-speed synchromesh gear-boxes and immediately Strachans made a 20-seat bus version available. Other builders also built on it, while Alexander (qv) built an integral midibus on Ford A-series units. Although Ford had high hopes for the A-series it had a limited appeal and production ended in the early 1980s.

The end of the R-series and A-series did not, however, spell the end of Ford in the psv market; the Transit was about to come into the ascendancy. The Ford Transit had become virtually the standard minibus for the limited amount of minibus work

which was required prior to bus deregulation. However, in 1984, in the run-up to deregulation, Devon General placed a number of Transits in service in Exeter, replacing large buses on wide headways with a fast, frequent hail-&-ride operation. The rest, as they say, is history; the Ford Transit was to revolutionise the provision of local bus services and soon became a familiar sight on bus services nearly everywhere. Perhaps a bit basic, with a slightly raucous 2.5litre direct-injection diesel engine, the smallest di engine available at the time, it proved a terrific workhorse with capacity for much harder work and longevity than anyone had imagined. Some of those early Devon General ones clocked up 10 years' service, and intensive urban bus work was probably the harshest environment the versatile Transit was to encounter. Most were 16-seaters, though it was found possible to increase capacity to 20. This proved counter-productive; as the Transit was so close to its design weight at 20 seats, no standees could be carried, so the 20-seater actually had less carrying capacity than the 16-seater.

A new, more stylish VE6 model was introduced in 1986, though NBC took large quantities of the old model as Ford ran out the last ones, such that the

VE6, though very common in other applications, was
never to became so familiar as a psv; by the time it
came on stream for psv work the Transit had become
a victim of its own success; 16-seaters were now too
small. Only the Badgerline and Transit Holdings
groups took to the new model to any extent, in the
case of the latter with a purpose-built body by Mellor,
which with its rather tall dimensions looked ungainly
but was remarkably practical and gave probably the
best passenger environment of any Transit body. The
Transit is of course still very much available, and
increases in sophistication all the time. It now boasts
independent front suspension and fancy electronic
engine controls are available. However, as a minibus
it is back in its traditional rôle for welfare and
specialist psv applications.

Freight Rover/LDV

Perhaps a slightly unusual entry, Freight Rover
enjoyed a brief vogue as a major supplier of minibus
chassis as an alternative to the much more successful
and reliable Ford Transit in the mid-1980s. The
Freight Rover Sherpa began life as one of the British
Leyland Group's less auspicious products, the
successor to a number of different Austin and Morris
models, introduced in 1971. It was built in what had
been the BMC van plant in Birmingham, a stone's
throw from the MCW plant in Washwood Heath.

It was not used to any great extent as a psv chassis
until the time of deregulation when National Bus
Company in particular needed large quantities of 16-
20-seat minibuses, and it was just at a time when Ford

and Mercedes-Benz were changing over models. This
provided an entry into the market for Freight Rover,
and over 1,000 Sherpas went into NBC service in
1986/87, mainly with Carlyle bodywork. Indeed,
following the parcel-van style of body, Carlyle developed its rather more stylish Carlyle II specifically for
the Sherpa. Other customers included Yorkshire
Rider, which took it in a form converted from the
panel van by Optare, and a deregulation newcomer,
Bee Line Buzz, which launched a fleet of 160 of them
into the Manchester area in January 1987. The Sherpa
was never as reliable as the Transit, and both were
superseded on minibus work by bigger vehicles very
quickly. Some operators, notably Lincolnshire Road
Car, got round the reliability problem by fitting Ford
Transit engines and gearboxes.

Freight Rover went with Leyland Trucks to DAF
and became Leyland-DAF Vans. Following the
collapse of the Leyland-DAF company a management
buy-out was undertaken, and the company continues
as LDV, the larger versions of the Sherpa now being
the 400, using Peugeot engines. A replacement for the
Sherpa, jointly with Renault, was lost in the process,
but the 400 still soldiers on and is used by Royal Mail
as the standard postbus. It also crops up in small
numbers as the basis of minicoaches.

Guy

Wolverhampton-based Guy Motors had not been a significant bus producer before the war, though in 1941 it and Leyland were appointed to build a range of standardised Utility double-deck buses, initially 500 apiece. In the event Leyland concentrated on other military work, leaving Guy to produce its 500 Arab Is, before Daimler was appointed as the other wartime supplier in 1942. Bristol followed on later. Daimler's CWG5 and CWA6 were based on its prewar models, and also built in a factory allocated to it in Wolverhampton. The Arab I in standard form

was powered by the Gardner 5LW, though a small number had 6LWs requiring the front end to be extended — and in fact putting the bus over the legal length at the time. Nonetheless the Arab II adopted the extended front end, regardless of which engine was fitted.

Guy's experience of wartime production meant that it emerged into the postwar period as one of the major players in the bus business, and indeed the Utility Arab II continued in production until early-1946, despite the fact that other manufacturers had already been given the go-ahead for their postwar ranges. However, by this time the wartime specification was

Right:
London Transport specified its own version of the Guy Vixen for lightly-used country area services. GS13 is still in service with London & Country, one of the successors to London Transport's Country Bus & Coach division. They had ECW bodywork.

Below:
The concealed radiator is more readily identified with the Guy Arab IV; this 30ft model with Northern Counties bodywork was new to Lancashire United in 1958.

Above:
Lancashire United was also a major user of the forward entrance Arab V; this one, seen on the trunk Manchester-Bolton service, was new in 1965.
R. L. Wilson

Above right:
The Wulfrunian, with its front engine on the front platform and a host of innovative features was a factor in Guy's downfall. West Riding was the driving force behind the design and its main customer, mainly with Roe bodywork.

relaxed a little, allowing some light alloys to be used in its construction, and a polished aluminium radiator surround in place of the austere painted unit of the true Utilities. The rather basic Arab proved a reliable and durable chassis and many were rebodied or at least refurbished after the war and gave 20 or more years' service. Over 2,500 had been built during the war.

Guy's first postwar model was the Arab III, introduced in 1946. It continued the theme of the wartime Arabs, though available as a single-decker as well as a double-decker, and featured a lower bonnet and radiator line. A new engine alternative was offered from 1948, the 10.35litre Meadows 6DC630, though despite offering larger capacity than the 8.4litre Gardner 6LW it was something of an unknown quantity, and found few takers. It was deleted in 1951. One user was London Transport, which specified the engine in a one-off Arab III with Guy's own bodywork to a sort of pseudo-RT style. This also had the preselective gearbox offered as an option from 1948. The same gearbox, though with Gardner 6LW engine, was specified by Birmingham City Transport in a new model built initially to Birmingham's specification, the Arab IV. Birmingham's first ones arrived in 1950, with concealed radiators; Birmingham was multiple sourcing identical-looking buses from Daimler, Guy and Crossley at this time, and took 301 Arabs. Like

the wartime Arab these too proved very long-lived, lasting up to 25 years and being used by West Midlands PTE to see off rather newer trolleybuses in Walsall.

The Arab IV was offered generally from 1951, with a new constant-mesh gearbox and an option of an exposed radiator, while the Arab III remained on the market until 1953, partly — though by no means exclusively — to fulfil requirements for halfcab single-deckers. Guy had come from nowhere before the war to being the standard bus for a good many operators, notably smaller municipalities such as Chester, Darlington and Blackburn, though it was also taken up enthusiastically by larger operators such as Belfast, Southampton and its home town, Wolverhampton, while company operators taking to

the type included East Kent, Lancashire United, Southdown, Northern General and some of the Scottish Bus Group companies. Most Arab IVs had Gardner 6LW engines, though Moores of Kelvedon for one specified 5LWs in 30ft vehicles, which must have been decidedly slow, but in 1958 the Arab IV became the first to offer Gardner's new 10.45litre 6LX.

Meanwhile Guy offered quite a wide range of single-deckers, including a range of lightweights, some normal control. Perhaps the most famous of the latter were the 84 Vixen Specials built for London Transport in 1953, with ECW bodywork and Ford-styled fronts, which formed the GS class. However, before the war Guy had offered two small single-deck models, the normal-control 20-seat Wolf and forward-control 30-seat Vixen, production of which, with a new radiator resembling that of the Arab, resumed in 1947. A heavier 30-seat Otter was offered from 1950, with a choice of Gardner 4LK or, later, Perkins P6, as options to the 58bhp 3.7litre petrol engine also fitted to the Vixen. The Wolf had a smaller, 3.3litre 50bhp petrol unit.

Underfloor-engined versions of the Arab for single-deck use appeared in 1950, offering a horizontal Gardner engine and preselector or constant-mesh gearbox, with a lighter-weight LUF replacing Arab III single-deckers from 1952. The LUF remained in production until 1959, though did not sell in large quantities. Meanwhile a new front-engined chassis, the Warrior, was built for overseas markets as a replacement for the Arab III single-decker, and an underfloor-engined version of this was developed which sold a few in this country. It offered a wider range of engines than the Arab LUF, including AEC and Meadows.

It was unfortunate that Guy, with its origins in straightforward, robust engineering should stray from that path when it came to developing a vehicle for the new vogue of front-entrance double-deckers heralded by the Leyland Atlantean. The placing of well-tried components in a package across the back of the bus, with recourse to angle drives, was not an immediate or universal success, so there was some logic in developing an alternative with a more straightforward drive line. The idea was the brainchild of West Riding's chief engineer, Ron Brooke, who was also keen to try different suspension systems to counteract the problems of rough roads in his company's operating area. Other manufacturers had turned down the idea, but Guy agreed to develop it.

The Wulfrunian appeared in 1959. It featured a Gardner 6LX engine mounted ahead of the front wheels with the entrance alongside it. It also had other advanced features for the time, all items from which Leyland had fought shy with the Atlantean, such as air suspension, independent at the front, and disc brakes. Maybe a more conservative design utilising the same basic concept might have worked, though even that is doubtful; the Gardner 6LX owed much of its reliability to solid construction and generous specification, and as a result was a big beast which took up too much room on the platform, resulting in a cramped entrance, compared with Leyland's excellent entrance arrangement on the Atlantean, necessitating a nearside staircase which was also cramped, and an equally cramped cab. Originally Guy had intended to offer the Gardner 6LW, Leyland and AEC engines in the Wulfrunian.

The front-mounted engine also gave the bus very poor weight distribution (emphasised by the strange toe-out attitude afforded to the front wheels by the independent suspension). In later years West Riding had to take out the upstairs front seats to alleviate the problem of tyre wear.

The Wulfrunian took up a huge amount of sparse cash reserves in its development and did not sell, other than to West Riding, which took 127 from 1960 to 1965. Only 10 others were built, for Bury, Lancashire United, County Motors, West Wales, Accrington — which oddly had them with rear entrances and a short front overhang, rather negating the whole purpose of the Wulfrunian, and Wolverhampton, which also had one with a short overhang though forward entrance. By 1961 the company was bankrupt, and was bought by Jaguar, now the owner of Daimler.

Under Jaguar ownership a new version of the Arab emerged in 1962, the Mark V, available in 27ft or 30ft versions. It had a lower chassis frame than the Arab IV and was thus better suited to forward-entrance applications than its predecessor, though it appeared in both forward and rear-entrance forms.

Although a conservative design, it remained in production, apart from a short break in the 27ft model when Daimler's CCG6, with a Guy constant-mesh gearbox, was offered in its place, until the end of half-cab bus production in this country; the last went to Chester in 1969, one of a only a handful of H-registered half-cab buses.

Guy, by now owned by British Leyland, continued in the export market, but production was transferred to Leyland in 1982 and the Wolverhampton factory was closed.

Harrington

Hove-based Harrington was one of the most highly-respected coachbuilders in postwar Britain, with a fine range of bodies bought particularly, though by no means exclusively, by the BET Group companies. It also built a smaller number of competent bus bodies, and like Beadle, Harrington, which had a Rootes car dealership in Hove, saw the opportunities presented by Commer's underfloor-engined concept for an integral single-decker with the entrance ahead of the front axle. Thus in 1953 it produced an integral coach, the Contender, using the petrol engine from the Avenger. However, later ones used the two-stroke TS3 diesel. BOAC bought 12 Contender coaches between 1953 and 1958, the last three with Rolls-Royce petrol engines and automatic transmission. It did not sell in large numbers, though Maidstone & District bought 11 with 42-seat bus bodywork and TS3 engines in 1955.

Harrington also built integral minibuses based on Ford 4D running units. They had up to 19 seats, but many went to BOAC as 12-seaters.

Right:
A Commer-powered Harrington Contender coach of 1953.

Jensen

This West Bromwich firm is generally remembered for its exotic sports cars, and the Interceptor of the late 1960s was one of the all-time classics in British sports cars. Nevertheless it did dabble into the commercial vehicle business in the late 1940s/early 1950s, under the JNSN tag which came from the characteristic use of these initials as a cut out for the radiator. Its specialism was integrally-built vehicles, mainly pantechnicons. However, it did branch out in a small way into passenger vehicles, with a lightweight 40-seater using a Perkins P6 engine and David Brown five-speed gearbox. It was introduced in 1949 and had a body structure by Sparshatts. A 38-seat luxury version came out at only 5tons 3cwt unladen, but it failed to catch on.

Jensen made another attempt in the psv market in 1958, with a remarkable 13-seat minibus, the Tempo 1500. This was built under licence from a German manufacturer, Tempo, but for this UK application was fitted with a BMC 1.5litre B-series petrol engine mounted back-to-front under the floor at the front and driving the front wheels via a ZF four-speed gearbox. The vehicle was also available as a van.

Below:
A Jensen integral bus, showing the Sparshatts tubular construction for the body. Note the 'JNSN' emblem forming a grille.

Bottom:
The Jensen Tempo 14-seat minibus with Austin petrol engine, seen at Earls Court in 1958.

Karrier

Karrier was best-known as a bus producer up to the mid-1930s when it was taken over by the Rootes Group, in 1934, after which production was transferred from Huddersfield to the Commer factory at Luton. Thereafter it concentrated on smaller, lightweight vehicles, effectively the smaller end of the Commer range. Its main model throughout the 1950s was the Bantam, which was available as an attractive 14-seat Reading-bodied coach, notable for its faired-in rear wheels. It had a four-cylinder 48bhp engine.

A few Commer Walkthru van derivatives used as minibuses were sold as Karriers.

Leyland

It still seems incredible that Leyland is no longer with us. At one time, when Volvo was still an insignificant Swedish also-ran, it was the world leader in bus and coach production. It had markets all over the world and by the end of the 1960s had mopped up the entire heavyweight bus production of this country. Yet by 1993 it had all gone, with just vestiges of it showing in certain Volvo models. If one discounts the engineering legacy which can be found in the products of numerous manufacturers throughout the world, that is.

But before we get too gloomy about the present we must return to 1945, when Leyland was just returning to bus production after an enforced rest. A rest that is from building buses; instead Leyland was a major producer for the war effort and as mentioned above, although it was intended that Leyland should build buses during the war that didn't come about, once it had finished assembling chassis for which it already had parts.

Its postwar range was launched at the end of 1945, and comprised two solid but unremarkable models, the Titan PD1 double-decker and mechanically identical Tiger PS1 single-decker. They followed on from prewar models, though with the 7.4litre E101 engine that had been developed for military use during the war and a redesigned front end which was to set the standard for postwar production. They had four-speed constant-mesh gearboxes, vacuum brakes and were quite conventional. They were followed in 1947 by the PD2 and PS2 models, which were undoubtedly Leyland's most successful models ever. These used the new 9.8litre 125bhp O.600 engine, on which much of Leyland's postwar success was built, coupled to a synchromesh four-speed gearbox, which was less successful. Indeed this had to be reworked, with a new version with synchromesh only on the top two gears, which settled down to be Leyland's standard gearbox for the next 20 years, and some PD2s reverted to crash gearboxes while this was being undertaken.

The PD2 was to remain in the catalogue for 20 years, and appeared in numerous guises, 7ft 6in and 8ft wide, with vacuum brakes or air brakes, with manual gearboxes, semi-automatic gearboxes and even preselectors, with conventional exposed radiators or with two types of concealed radiator. It was developed into the slightly heavier export version, the OPD2 (also sold in Ireland), up till 1954 it could be obtained as a complete vehicle with Leyland's own competently-styled body or bodied by other concerns, and it even spawned a special version for London which was virtually a Leyland-built RT chassis, in 7ft 6in wide RTL form or 8ft wide and bodied by Leyland as the RTW. Nominally these were respectively PD2/1 and PD2/3 versions, although they shared little in common with provincial versions of the same chassis, other than the O.600 engine and the axles. They had AEC preselector gearboxes, air brakes and a low bonnet and radiator style which was virtually the same as the AEC version, though without the famous Blue Triangle, of course.

In 1956 the PD2 was joined by the mechanically identical PD3, which was 30ft long, and shared all the same variants as the PD2. The Titan sold in huge quantities mainly to municipal and BET fleets in this country, though PD1s had also appeared with THC fleets before they were tied too securely to Bristol, and also sold well abroad. The Tiger PS2 was no less competent, but was rendered obsolescent, not least by Leyland's own other endeavours in the single-deck department.

Meanwhile Leyland had been looking at underfloor-engined single-deckers. It had produced a batch for London Transport before the war, though still with the front axle in the normal position. A horizontal version of the O.600 engine was shown at the 1948 Commercial Motor Show, and details also emerged of an integral frame by MCW for an underfloor-engined Leyland. This appeared in 1949 as the HR40 Olympic, 40 designating the seating capacity. When length regulations were relaxed in 1951 to allow 30ft single-deckers on two axles it became the HR44, a 44-seater. However, the market was still reluctant to accept integral buses, and the Olympic was a pretty heavy bus anyway so showed little advantage as an integral, so the same components were fitted into a separate chassis, the Royal Tiger, from 1950. In the event all home-market ones were 30ft long, though there was a choice of 7ft 6in or 8ft width, air or vacuum brakes and a rear extension to support the boot on coach versions. Like the Olympic, it was a heavy bus and in 1952 the lighter-weight Tiger Cub was introduced, with the smaller, 5.7litre O.350 engine, which was similar to that fitted into the normal-control Comet, basically a lorry range but available as a passenger vehicle of the Bedford OB school. The Tiger Cub had a constant-mesh gearbox and air brakes, and from 1953 the same components were available in another MCW-built integral, the

Above:
London's own version of the Leyland Titan PD2 was the RTL; RTL1176 is seen here prior to setting off to New York on a 'Come to Britain' tour in 1964.

Right:
The combination of Leyland's own bodywork and concealed radiator was a very rare one, specified by Midland Red to resemble its own products on 100 PD2/20s bought in 1953 as its class LD8. Two are seen in Coventry in 1955.
W. H. R. Godwin

Olympian, though this met with rather less success than the Olympic had enjoyed. The Tiger Cub however, sold very well, and later larger O.375 and O.400 engines were offered, as were Albion five-speed gearboxes.

The heavier single-deckers were effectively phased-out; although the Tiger PS2 continued for export as the OPS2, home-market production ended in 1954, and in the same year the Royal Tiger became the Worldmaster, also intended for export though some were sold in this country. The Olympic too was developed as an overseas model.

The next single-deck chassis with the O.600 engine was the Leopard L1, which was shown at the 1959 Scottish Motor Show. This was rather lighter in weight than the Royal Tiger, though mechanically similar. However, it was built as standard with air brakes. The L2 was a coach version, with a more powerful, faster-revving version of the same engine and a rear frame extension. 36ft versions became available in 1961, as the PSU3, and the Leopard steadily developed as Leyland's main coach model, gaining Pneumocyclic semi-automatic transmission and the larger O.680 engine over the years. As Leyland took over various other heavyweight manu-facturers it was to become the only British heavy-weight coach, available in 12m form as well as 11m and 10m, and became the standard National Bus

Company and Scottish Bus Group coach. Ulsterbus too standardised on it for bus and coach work. Production was finally replaced by the Tiger in 1982, by which time the Leopard was showing its age quite seriously. A hybrid model, heavier than the Leopard but less heavy than the Worldmaster was the 33ft-long Royal Tiger Cub. Intended for export it was also bought by Doncaster Corporation.

Returning to the 1950s, Leyland was looking at alternatives for double-deckers, largely with a view to increasing seating capacity. The first rear-engined double-deck prototype was built in 1952. Named the Lowloader it had a body by Saunders-Roe, showing distinct similarities to the body developed by that

company for the Tiger Cub. A turbocharged O.350 engine was fitted on the rear platform; apart from a trolleybus-style full front the layout of the bus was entirely conventional, with open rear platform, and the O.350 was chosen for its small dimensions. The structure was semi-integral, with an underframe incorporating wheelarches etc and it had independent front suspension. A second prototype, using a similar underframe though bodied with a half-cab body by MCW followed two years later. However, the third prototype was built in 1956, by which time 30ft double-deckers could be built on two axles. Thus the entrance was moved to the front, ahead of the front axle, which not only gave driver supervision of the platform but also left more room for the engine at the rear, so the trusty O.600 could be used instead. The integral, low-height prototype still used independent front suspension, and the underframe included the entire floor structure. The body was built by MCW and the whole was named the Atlantean.

However, the complex construction of the Atlantean was found to create various drawbacks, and there was customer resistance from the likes of BET, which didn't like to be tied to one bodybuilder, so when the production Atlantean was launched in 1958 it reverted to a conventional chassis frame, beam front axle and a straight rear axle dictating a normal height. Bodywork was initially by MCW, though other

builders were soon able to build on it and despite the fact that its main advantage over a PD3 was an increase in capacity of only five seats at the most it sold remarkably well. Within 10 years it had seen off the conventional front-engined chassis, though by this time one-person operation of double-deckers had been legalised, so it offered obvious advantages. Indeed during the early 1960s there was something of a backlash against the concept; early operators got their fingers burnt with unreliability and found little advantage, so returned to conventional buses. Ironically many of those early Atlantean users worked hard to get their vehicles working properly and eventually got very good, long service out of them.

As one-person operation became the norm, so improvements were necessary for the Atlantean, and an improved AN68 version was introduced in 1972. This used the O.680 engine as standard (it had been an option on the earlier, PDR-series), and also had standard power steering, spring brakes etc as well as a lengthened rear overhang to accommodate back-to-back seating over the rear wheelarch as had become popular. In this form the Atlantean was a remarkable success, overcoming most of the unreliability of early models. It remained in production until 1984, outlasting later newcomers, the Daimler Fleetline and Bristol VRT. Although Leyland had had plans to replace its entire double-deck production with a single

Left:
A Ribble Leyland Royal Tiger coach with Leyland's own bodywork, seen in Rochdale.

Centre left:
The Comet was a popular medium-weight lorry, though appeared sometimes in bus and coach guise too, like this one for Mulleys, Ixworth.
M. A. Sutcliffe

Below:
Following the Royal Tiger was the lighter-weight Tiger Cub, suitable as both a bus or a coach. This Ribble one has Burlingham Seagull bodywork.

Right:
Leyland produced the first successful rear-engined double-decker, the Atlantean. Earlier ones had plain front ends, though by the time this one was bodied by MCW for Bournemouth in 1964 more style was being put into bodywork for them.

new model in the 1970s, as we shall see, it was European regulations which finally ended the Atlantean's 26-year run — with that O.680 engine it was just too noisy — by which time some 15,000 had been sold. It was the best-selling double-decker of all times.

Leyland's forays into rear-engined single-deckers were less successful. In 1962 Leyland had merged with ACV, and the same chassis was used as the basis of the Leyland Panther and the AEC Swift. Neither did much credit for their manufacturer, though oddly enough both types were highly regarded in Australia. The Panther and the Panther Cub were both launched in 1964, the former a 36ft chassis with the O.600 engine mounted horizontally at the rear, the latter 33ft with the O.400. The Panther was available with a stepped chassis frame as the PSUR1/1, for bus use, offering a very low entrance, or with a higher, straight frame as the PSUR1/2 for coach use, with the advantage of useful underfloor locker space. Most were built as buses however. Neither type was hugely successful, and once one-man operation of double-deckers was legalised from 1966 few operators persisted with it.

Much was about to change for Leyland. It had already acquired ACV, then in 1965 took a 25% stake in Bristol. In 1968, however, it was merged with the ailing British Motor Corporation to form British Leyland. BMC had acquired Jaguar two years earlier, so Daimler and Guy also joined the Leyland stable. Problems now really began, as the car and commercial vehicle businesses did not coexist terribly happily. Both needed to invest in new models, and the commercial vehicle business lost out as money was invested in new car ranges; and even these were hardly the cream of the European automotive industry, resulting in models such as the Austin Allegro and Morris Marina. Another effect was that production of Daimler's last model, the Fleetline, was moved from Coventry to Leyland in 1973 to make room for increased production of Jaguar cars. The name was changed to the Leyland Fleetline at the end of 1974 and production ended in 1980.

A joint venture was set up with the new National Bus Company in 1969. Leyland and NBC became equal partners in Bristol, and also set up a whole new organisation, Leyland National, to build a brand new integral rear-engined single-decker on mass-production lines in a brand new factory at Workington. The integral construction was such that many of the structural problems which had bedevilled the first generation of rear-engined single-deckers were overcome, especially as the new structure was jig-built, allowing semi-skilled labour to produce a precision job.

Leyland had been working on a radical four-axle Commuterbus, which might have brought low-floor buses in by the 1970s rather than the 1990s, and while the Leyland National stopped short of that it was still quite radical. Leyland had developed a new fixed-head engine, the 500, and a horizontal, turbocharged version of this 8.2litre unit was used in the new bus. Although its 200bhp plus output was impressive, as was its free-revving character, it was not to be the most reliable of units and the installation in the Leyland National meant it was rather prone to smoke too. However, the corrosion-protected steel structure of the bus was rather more successful and proved to be remarkably strong and durable. Being mass-produced there was little operator choice; features such as destination boxes, seats etc were all standardised, though there was a choice of single or double doors and 10.3m or 11.3m length. Air suspension was standard as was a five-speed Pneumocyclic gearbox, with semi- or fully-automatic control.

National Bus Company adopted it as its standard single-decker and quickly took large quantities, which was just as well; once one-person operation of double-deckers was unexpectedly legalised in 1966 the writing was on the wall for rear-engined single-deckers. However, the bus industry was falling into a very bleak period, with long delays in fulfilling orders and many operators took readily-available Leyland Nationals rather than wait for something more to their liking. Nonetheless ambitious production forecasts

needed to offset the high capital cost in setting up the highly automated factory were never met. The Leyland National was first exhibited at the 1970 Commercial Motor Show, and soon started appearing in large numbers on the roads. It went through a number of modifications before a Mark 2 model was introduced in 1979. This used the O.680 engine and moved the radiator to the front, extending the bus by 0.3m and giving rise to a rather bulbous snout, which spoilt the clean lines of the original design. Options of Gardner and Leyland TL11 engines were offered later, but the days of large-scale purchases of new buses were over and the National 2 never reached the sort of volumes enjoyed by the earlier model. They drifted downwards until production ground to a halt in 1984.

Leyland also had similar ideas for the double-deck market. With the Leyland National it had virtually wiped out all opposition in the single-deck citybus market, and during the 1970s plans were hatched for a new integral double-decker to do the same. A highly-sophisticated new bus emerged as the B15 in 1975, at a time when British Leyland was struggling to such an extent that the Government had had to step in to rescue it in 1974. When the B15 eventually got into production it was named the Titan. Though prototypes had the Leyland 500-series engine and it was then expected that the replacement for the O.680, the TL11, would be used, the Gardner 6LXB engine became standard with a hydraulically operated auto-

Left:
The AN68 version of the Atlantean was produced from 1972. This Alexander-bodied vehicle began life with Grampian but later passed to Midland Bluebird, after it came into Grampian ownership.

Right:
The Leyland Leopard was a popular choice for coach work from its introduction in 1959, and it was one of the first types available for 36ft-long coaches. This early 36-footer has Plaxton Panorama bodywork for Yorkshire Woollen District.

Centre right:
The Leopard also made a popular high-capacity single-deck bus, especially with BET companies. With typical BET-style Willowbrook dual-purpose bodywork is Midland Red 6398, one of that operator's class S24 of 1971.

Below:
The combination of Leyland Leopard chassis and Plaxton Panorama Elite bodywork was probably the classic coach of the early 1970s. This one, new in 1974, belonged to Lancashire United.
R. L. Wilson

Top:
ECW produced its rather unsuccessful B51 coach body for the Leopard and Tiger in the early-1980s. This Leopard was new to Hants & Dorset, remaining with Hampshire Bus and passing with it to Stagecoach South's Coastline operation.

Above:
The rugged construction of the Leopard meant that it became a popular basis for rebuilding as service buses once it had become outmoded for coach use. Willowbrook did a brisk trade in such rebuilding, with its functional looking Warrior body.
Kevin Lane

Top right:
However comprehensive a manufacturer's catalogue was, someone always wanted something different. So when Leyland introduced the Panther Manchester Corporation wanted something smaller. Regulations governing the relationship of overhangs to overall length meant that the O.600 engine was too big, so the Panther Cub used essentially Tiger Cub running units in a Panther-style rear-engined chassis. They had attractive Park Royal bodywork of a style also supplied on Panther chassis in some quantity to Stockholm.

Right:
One of the first of several thousand production Leyland Nationals was this one for Crosville.

Above:
The Leyland 500-series engine in the Leyland National was often considered its worst feature, so Leyland introduced the National 2 in 1979, with an O.680 engine, which necessitated moving the radiator to the front. This resulted in a 0.3m bulge at the front, detracting from the clean lines of the original design. This one went to Eastern Scottish; Scottish Bus Group had been a less than enthusiastic user of the original Leyland National. Mull is an area of Airdrie, rather than the better known island.
Iain MacGregor

Left:
Carrying Leyland decals is a late-model Fleetline of Chester, running on hire to Maidstone in 1986.
David Jenkins

Below left:
A Workington-built Leyland Titan working for London Coaches. It was new to London Transport.

matic gearbox, the Hydracyclic, air suspension, independent at the front, and a low, flat floor. Small numbers were built with Leyland TL11 engines. The Bristol VRT had been used in its Mark 3 form as a proving ground for an advanced cooling system which enabled the engine to be encapsulated for very low noise levels, and in terms of noise and ride quality it was an impressive performer.

However, Leyland's plans to make the Titan the sole, standard double-deck bus were thwarted. Industrial relations problems surrounded its efforts to get it into production, such that large orders outside London were lost, and the threat both to bodybuilders, faced with starvation of chassis, and dismay amongst operators being denied their traditional element of choice led to a rise in new rival manufacturers. Production eventually got going at Park Royal, which

had become part of the Leyland empire through the merger with ACV, but further industrial problems there led to the closure of the plant after 250 London Titans, plus smaller numbers for Greater Manchester, West Midlands and Reading, had been built and production continued at Workington, where there was excess capacity. It too ground to a halt in 1985 after less than 1,200 had been produced.

Leyland also saw that it needed to offer a double-deck chassis, so Titan components were arranged in a separate frame, similar in many respects to the Bristol VRT, to produce the Olympian. Unlike the Titan this had a beam axle at the front, with a clever arrangement of outboard air bellows to give a low entrance, and a dropped-centre rear axle to enable low-height bodywork to be built on it. It had a bolted perimeter frame chassis and engine options at this stage were

Above:
Leyland launched the Tiger in 1981 in grand style in Morocco, hence the exotic background to this Eastern Scottish coach with characteristic Duple Dominant III bodywork.

Right:
Ulsterbus was a keen user of Leyland Tigers for service bus work; indeed for several years it was the standard Northern Irish bus. This one has Alexander (Belfast) Q-type bodywork.

Left:
London Country took Leyland Tigers with high-floor Berkhof bodywork for Green Line use in 1985. The first is seen at the official launch at Gatwick Airport.

Centre left:
Leyland's response to the influx of Continental integral coaches was the stylish rear-engined Royal Tiger Doyen. Reliance of Gravesend is a keen user of the type.
Kevin Lane

Below:
The Royal Tiger was also available as a separate underframe; this one, delivered to Jacobs, Southampton, in 1984, has Van Hool bodywork.

Above right:
The Cub was a small, front-engined chassis based on the Terrier truck. Though used extensively for welfare and local-authority work some were used as psvs; Southdown used this one with Reeve Burgess bodywork on County Rider services in East Sussex. They had wheelchair lifts at the rear and combined local bus operation with various social services and health service functions.

Right:
With typical ECW bodywork is a Crosville Wales Leyland Olympian, seen in Chester in 1987.
Kevin Lane

the Gardner 6LXB or Leyland TL11. Production began at the Bristol factory in 1981, and was moved to Workington when Bristol was closed the next year. Some production went to Leyland in 1985, and by 1987 all Olympians were being built there before production moved back to Workington in 1990.

Meanwhile Leyland had had to address the coach market, where the aged Leopard was losing ground to the importers. It was replaced from 1981 (though production continued until the next year) by the Tiger, which had a more powerful turbocharged TL11 engine, giving 218bhp, coupled to a choice of Hydracyclic or ZF manual gearboxes, and full air suspension. It was an impressive chassis compared to the Leopard, and in later life 245bhp and 260bhp versions of the TL11 engine were offered. The next year an even more impressive coach was launched, resuming the Royal Tiger name, and this was built at the Charles H. Roe body plant. It used similar compo-

nents to the Tiger but with the engine at the rear and employing a complex space frame which could be bodied by other builders or take Roe's own Doyen body, which featured bonded glazing and styling which was completely up to date with the rear-engined integrals coming in particularly from Germany. Whereas the Tiger quickly settled down as a reliable workhorse the Royal Tiger was a bit more temperamental and certainly didn't match its German rivals for build quality. Only 60 Royal Tigers were built at Roe, 41 of them bodied there, before production moved to Workington in 1984.

Development work had been progressing only slowly on the replacement for the Leyland National; as single-deck volumes were so low it was hardly a pressing priority. A prototype underframe had been built in 1983, and a few more were built in 1985/86, including a small batch to be bodied by Alexander (Belfast) for Ulsterbus and Citybus. The Lynx offered

Top:
The Stagecoach Group standardised on long-wheel-base Olympians with Alexander bodywork. This early example is seen in Chichester.

Above:
Stagecoach also took three Hong Kong-style three-axle Olympians.
G. H. F. Atkins

a choice of TL11 or Gardner engines with ZF automatic transmission, and later the Cummins L10 was also offered. Meanwhile a very box-like body with flat bonded glass was developed for it, lacking much of the style of the Leyland National and also the structural competence of it. Nevertheless sales did pick up by the end of the 1980s, largely through large orders from West Midlands, Badgerline and Caldaire.

By now Leyland was into a new regime. Margaret Thatcher's Government which had come to power in 1979 was determined to take organisations like British Leyland out of the state sector. As a result the company was split into various separate businesses and Leyland Bus was finally sold to its management on 13 January 1987. This could scarcely have been a worse time for its new owners as bus orders had slumped nationwide in the wake of the restructuring of the operating industry. However, they managed to introduce one new model, the mid-engined Swift midibus, based on the Roadrunner lorry chassis, though this provided a much less suitable urban midibus than the Dennis Dart, which was mechanically very similar with a Cummins B-series engine, Allison transmission and parabolic steel suspension, was later to prove. The Swift had replaced a rather less acceptable, similar-sized front-engined chassis, the Cub, which had a Perkins engine and was used primarily for welfare and schools use. The Inner London Education Authority was a particularly large user, though some were built for psv use.

The Lynx was now established and the Olympian had always enjoyed a good reputation while the Tiger was holding its own, especially since the splitting up of Leyland, leading to the phasing-out of Leyland's engine production, meant that Leyland Bus was now fitting the well-respected Cummins L10 engine and giving it power outputs up to 290bhp. The L10 also became the standard power unit for both the Olympian and the Lynx, using ZF automatic transmission; Leyland by this time was producing parts for ZF. However, longer-term investment in research and development was going to be difficult with such low volumes and lack of major backing, and so on 30 March 1988 Leyland Bus was sold to Volvo.

Volvo had great plans for Leyland, including the development of the Lynx for world markets and production of the B10M at Workington, although it promptly ended production of the Royal Tiger. A new joint sales organisation, VL Bus & Coach, took over Leyland's sales from 1 January 1989, but by 1 July 1991 further integration took place under the Volvo Bus Ltd name. By the end of that year Volvo decided enough was enough and having sustained substantial losses over the Leyland business pulled the plug on 6 December 1991. The closure of Leyland's last manufacturing plant, Workington, was announced as was the end of the Tiger and Lynx, with only the Olympian to continue as a Volvo. However, it took until July 1993 to close down Workington, as there were large run-out orders for the Leyland Olympian.

Above:
The Leyland Swift was developed from the Roadrunner truck chassis, though with mid-underfloor engine, the Cummins B-series in vertical format, during Leyland's independent period. It was soon eclipsed by the Dennis Dart, using the same driveline components in a more 'user-friendly' form. Many Swifts were bodied by Wadham Stringer, such as this Luton & District vehicle.
Kevin Lane

Below:
Leyland valediction. Two of the last Leylands built are this United Olympian with Alexander bodywork and Cleveland Transit Lynx 2, which, like the National 2, gained a bulge at the front to accommodate the radiator, in this case to fit in the intercooler for the Volvo engine which was later offered as an option. They are seen together in Stockton in August 1994.
Kevin Lane

Maudslay

Maudslay was a very old-established engineering firm based in Alcester, Warwickshire. Some of its prewar bus and coach designs showed some interesting innovation, but its postwar Marathon II and III single-deck coach chassis were highly conventional. The Marathon II was announced in 1946, and very quickly found a good following from independent coach operators in the main. It was conservative to the point of having a petrol engine, a rare example of a postwar heavyweight being so fitted, but sold 120 in about two years. It had a 7.4litre six-cylinder petrol engine with a unit-mounted five-speed gearbox, with direct-drive top, and was noted for its smoothness, with the combination of petrol engine and a high-geared rear axle.

The Marathon III was introduced at the beginning of 1947, with a diesel engine, though rather than develop its own suitable diesel Maudslay fitted the well-tried AEC 7.7litre diesel engine (actually 7.58litre, but always known as the 7.7) coupled to a four-speed AEC sliding-mesh gearbox. Production of both models continued side by side, though the Marathon III was by far the most successful postwar Maudslay. Again it was popular with independent operators, and sold around 600.

AEC was in something of an expansionist phase after the war, and in 1948, as it was already a supplier

Below:
A 1948 Duple-bodied Maudslay Marathon III demonstrator.

Bottom:
Rather an attractive 1948 Marathon III of Layfield Bus Services, Thornaby-on-Tees.

Above:
Full-front Metalcraft 37-seat bodywork was fitted to this
30ft-long, 8ft-wide Marathon III of Churchbridge Luxury
Coaches, Cannock. It was new in 1951.

of components to Maudslay, it bought the business.
This was the same year in which AEC bought
Crossley, and Associated Commercial Vehicles was
established as a parent company. Production of the
Marathon III continued until 1950.

That was not quite the end of the story for
Maudslay; AEC rather shamelessly performed 'badge
engineering' up to about 1956, largely to collar more
space at Commercial Motor Shows, and Regal IIIs,
Regent IIIs and even Reliances all appeared with the
Maudslay name, while some Regal IVs were built as
Maudslay Marathon IVs. Most were pure Southall
products, although a batch of nine Regent IIIs was
built for Coventry at the Alcester factory in 1950 and
were suitably badged. They entered service the
following January. Maudslay then became an axle
plant and also built AEC's dump trucks. It was sold
by Leyland in 1972 to the American-owned Rockwell
International as an axle manufacturer, and Rockwell
still builds axles and brake systems in Alcester.

Metro Cammell Weymann

Metro Cammell Weymann was originally the sales
organisation set up in 1932 to handle the separate
bodybuilding activities of Metropolitan Cammell,
based in Birmingham, and Weymann, of Addlestone,
Surrey. The two later joined forces as a single entity

and the Weymann factory closed in 1965. Although a
leading builder of separate bodywork, and a pioneer
of all-metal construction, MCW also had a long
history of building integral vehicles in conjunction
with Leyland; the Olympic came out in 1949, and
MCW also produced integral bodywork for the prototype Atlantean.

When it became apparent that Leyland was aiming
to produce its own integral vehicles for the 1970s,
effectively shutting the doors on the mainstream
bodybuilders, MCW decided to look for a partner
with which to build its own range of integral vehicles.
At the same time Swedish builder Scania-Vabis was
keen to break into the UK market, and so the two
agreed in 1969 for MCW to build the body structure
for what were effectively UK-market Scania CR111
integral vehicles. The Metro-Scania was something of
an advance for the UK, with full air suspension,
Scania's unusual two-speed fully-automatic transmission and performance which was rather more potent
than the norm for buses in Britain.

It gave the new Leyland National some competition, and actually got into the market before
Leyland's new products, in 1971. The Metro-Scania
remained in production only until 1973, by which
time 133 had been built, but MCW had developed a
double-deck version, the Metropolitan, which made
its debut at the 1973 Scottish Motor Show. This sold
rather more strongly; major orders were won from
some of the PTEs and London Transport, and 663 had
been sold by the time production ended in 1978.
MCW also built a one-off Scania-based coach in
1972, the Metropolitan 145, based on the V8-powered
Scania CR145.

MCW had been considering building its own

Above:
A typical London Mark 1 MCW Metrobus, M918, in Wimbledon in 1994.

Below:
A Mk 2 Metrobus in service with Maidstone & District at Tunbridge Wells in 1984.
John Marsh

integral since 1975. The Scania engine, for all its power, was considered thirsty, and there had also been problems with body corrosion. MCW had an agreement to build on Scania running units until 1979, but began serious work on its own integral in April 1976. It was to be a mainly alloy, semi-integral structure based on well-proven mechanical components, which involved the use of the Gardner 6LXB engine and Voith transmission, and full air suspension was used. The new vehicle was named Metrobus, and a demonstrator appeared in October 1977, followed by the first production bus, for West Midlands, which emerged the following January. This was closely followed by four more and five for London Transport. Both operators adopted it as a standard double-decker, almost exclusively so in the case of West Midlands, and dual-sourced with Leyland Titans in the case of London Transport. Between them they took more than 2,500 Metrobuses. It sold well both on the home market and overseas, and a Rolls Royce engine option was offered.

A new three-axle version was built for Hong Kong from 1981, and this had a revised body structure which was adapted to form the Mk 2 Metrobus for the home market from 1982. This superseded the original version, with its characteristic asymmetric windscreen (a feature it inherited from the Metro-Scania), although London Transport still specified the more expensive Mk 1 until it received its last in 1985.

MCW also branched out into other markets in 1982. At the Motor Show that year it showed an exotic three-axle double-deck coach in Scottish Citylink livery. It was the first time the new Citylink livery had been seen and it was also the first application in a British psv of the new Cummins L10 engine. Cummins had gained rather a bad reputation in the British bus industry which couldn't get on with the V6-200 fitted in the Daimler Roadliner (despite it faring rather better in other markets), though the new 10-litre L10 quickly gained a reputation for reliability, good performance and low fuel consumption, and was later to knock Gardner off its perch. The new coach, the Metroliner, used a 290bhp version of the engine, coupled to a Voith automatic transmission in a structure based on the Hong Kong Metrobus, though with bonded glazing and a much more stylish appearance. The standard of interior finish was impressive too, and for a manufacturer steeped in buses it stood up well against more established coach manufacturers. A single-deck version was also shown, again with the Cummins L10, though mounted in-line at the rear and driving through a ZF manual gearbox. Styling of this was rather more restrained, even uncompromisingly square. The single-deck version never caught on as well as the double-decker, despite a much-needed facelift, following the launch in 1983 of a high-floor Hiliner. Unlike the original single-deck Metroliner, this was fully integral; the original single-decker had a conventional chassis frame which intruded into the luggage space.

National Express had a large requirement for
double-decker coaches at this time. The Metroliner
had the drawback of being over 4m high, and therefore not suitable for Continental operation, which was
what most operators used double-deck coaches on.
National Express however, required the capacity of
the double-decker without needing it to go abroad,
and quickly ordered 39. It went on to order plenty
more and altogether 127 were built, all but 25 for
National Express. The single-decker only made it to
41, and ironically when MCW did get round to
producing a 4m double-decker, the Metroliner
400GT, with attractive styling and an in-line
Cummins 14-litre or Gardner 6LYT 15.5litre unit, it
sold only three.

MCW was developing a knack of producing new
products quickly to meet the demands of the market.
This had the drawback that they were not as reliable
as they might have been had a little more time been
spent getting out the bugs before production began.

This knack was also evident at the 1986 Show, when
MCW showed its first midibus, the 25-seat front-
engined Metrorider, the first integral vehicle aimed at
the post-deregulation minibus revolution. It offered
the choice of Perkins Phaser or Cummins B-series
four or six-cylinder engines of around one litre per
cylinder capacity, with a ZF manual or Allison automatic transmission. In the end virtually all orders
favoured the six-cylinder Cummins/Allison driveline.
Manual versions offered a new ceramic-lined clutch,
which wore well but took up too sharply for bus use.
Despite being pushed into production too quickly the
Metrorider sold like hot cakes, leaving some operators to repent at leisure when structural weaknesses,
especially round the back end, showed up.

It seems sales were also being gained rather too
cheaply at a time when the bus market was badly
depressed, and MCW's parent Laird Group was
concerned at the lack of profits coming in from
MCW. The Group considered that if it bought
Leyland Bus, which had come on to the market, with
the Government's desire to get British Leyland out of
the public sector, it would make a viable British bus
manufacturing business. In the end the Government
favoured Leyland's management buyout bid, and so
Laird Group decided to sell MCW at the end of 1988.
It proved a difficult business of which to dispose, and
it finished up, bit by bit, in the hands of Optare, which
reworked the Metrorider very effectively and reintroduced the Metrobus in a very different form.

Morris-Commercial

Morris was another manufacturer based in Birmingham. Before the war it had produced a range of purpose-designed heavyweight psvs, though it built no psv chassis from 1935 to 1948. Again that 1948 Commercial Motor Show was the venue for the launch of a 32-seat Morris-Commercial coach. It was a lightweight, though offered forward-control, and was powered by a Morris 4.25litre six-cylinder diesel engine, designed by Saurer, with the option of a 3.75litre four-cylinder petrol unit, driving through a four-speed manual gearbox. With the diesel engine it was known as type OP, and the petrol version was type PP.

It was largely an export chassis, though also sold in small numbers in this country. Thereafter Morris psvs were based on goods chassis, and the J2 of the late 1950s/early 1960s particularly sold, in both Austin and Morris forms, as a minibus.

Below:
A typical early postwar Morris-Commercial bus, of which little is known; it appears to be an export vehicle, probably a 1947 CVF13/5 with Wadham bodywork for Bermuda.

Bottom:
This rather attractive Mulliner-bodied Morris-Commercial was built in 1951 for the Morris Motors Band.

MORRIS MOTORS BAND

RFC 516

Moulton

Some time after Austin and Morris merged to become BMC it was decided to design a full-sized coach chassis to augment the large range of trucks. Work proceeded slowly, and was overtaken by events; BMC had become part of the enlarged Leyland empire and there was no longer any need for it.

But Moulton Developments subsequently completed and bodied a vehicle and put the design on the market in the early 1970s in the (unfulfilled) hope of finding a maker to buy the designs. The coach was an eight-wheeler, with twin steering axles at the front. Alex Moulton, of Hydrolastic suspension and Moulton Bicycle fame, was responsible for the design which provided superb riding and handling. The chassis had a Perkins 6.354 engine at the front, was of welded tube construction and weighed only 7,360kg when bodied. Most chassis parts came from the BMC-derived Leyland mid-weight truck range.

Northern General Transport

The major north-eastern bus operator Northern General had something of a history of building its own buses and coaches, some to very advanced design, prior to the war. After the war it built a few single-deckers using parts from prewar buses in a similar style to Beadle, in an effort to increase the number of 30ft vehicles in the fleet; Northern had probably the most intensive operation of any company operator. It was also obsessed with producing vehicles of light weight.

A bus and coach were built in 1951 to the maximum dimensions. The coach had a lengthened AEC Regal chassis, with a 7.7litre engine and preselector gearbox, and a new Picktree body, and 24 were built between 1951 and 1953.

The bus versions were probably more genuinely Northern General products, as they had 30ft x 8ft chassis frames fabricated by the company itself, and used 7.7litre engines and other components from 1936 AEC Regal IIs. Again they had Picktree bodies, designed by the operator, with an impressive 43 seats, only one less than the maximum possible in a contemporary underfloor-engined type which in the days before Tiger Cubs would have weighed considerably more than the 6ton 2cwt of the Northern vehicles. Only four were built and they were known as 'kipper boxes'.

In the 1970s Northern General also built its famous Tynesider and Wearsider double-deckers, which were heavy conversions respectively of a Leyland PD3 and a Routemaster for one-person operation. No more followed.

Below:
Two of Northern General's AEC-based 'Kipper Boxes' with a single-deck Guy Arab III.
M. A. Sutcliffe

Below right:
An Optare MetroRider in service in London.

Optare

Optare is something of a phenomenon! It was formed only in 1985, the worst time one could choose to come into the UK bus industry, and was a buyout of the former Leyland-owned Roe plant in Leeds. Leyland had closed it down in order to reduce body-building capacity in the face of slumping orders nationwide.

The new company made a very good showing, combining the experience and expertise of the Roe workforce and the flair of a brand new company. It was essentially a bodybuilder, but it offered its bodies as a complete product, with specific bodies married to specific chassis, which in some cases were not available for bodying by anyone else. In this respect Optare's main products can be regarded as complete vehicles, even if this is not literally true in an engineering sense.

Its first new model in this vein was the CityPacer, built on a Volkswagen LT55 chassis, specially imported for Optare's use and modified to suit Optare's design by the Leeds firm. It was introduced in 1986 as a 25-seater, at a time when 16-seat minibuses were still in vogue. However, the company had read the market well; the 25-seater was what the industry was on the verge of requiring, and unlike the 'breadvan' style of minibus the CityPacer had a refreshing and very distinctive styling which captured the imagination. It was followed by the bigger Mercedes-based StarRider.

Optare launched the full-sized Delta at the 1988 Birmingham Motor Show. It was based on the DAF SB220 chassis and marked the beginning of a relationship between DAF and Optare which was to have a profound bearing on the company's future direction. Like the CityPacer it had futuristic styling, and it used the Alusuisse system of bolted aluminium construction. At this stage the Delta was the only version of the SB220 available in Britain. The first went into service in February 1989 with Wigmores (Northern Bus), Sheffield, and production thereafter averaged about 70 a year.

As mentioned above MCW came on to the market at the end of 1988, and Optare bought the rights to produce the Metrorider. It reworked the bus to some extent, standardising on the turbocharged Cummins 6BT engine and Allison transmission. There was some restyling, and those structural weaknesses were ironed out. The interior styling came to resemble other Optare products, and the name was altered subtly to MetroRider in the style of its other midibus products. It remains in production and is Optare's only true integral. General opinion seems to be that it is now a much-improved product over the original MCW.

Optare also took over the rights to the Metrobus, but rather than putting it into production as such certain features were built into a new DAF chassis, the DB250, which was identical to the SB220 at the front but had a transverse engine and a driveline/rear suspension layout based on the Metrobus. Optare developed a new, very stylish Alusuisse body for it and it was launched in 1991 as the Spectra. In the

interim it had also started building a smaller single-decker based on the MAN 11.190 chassis, the Vecta.

Optare's ties with DAF had become stronger in July 1990 when it joined a new organisation, United Bus, which had been formed to build links between certain manufacturers in Europe. DAF Bus was the prime mover, but the Dutch bus market collapsed and United Bus went into receivership in 1993. Optare managed to buy itself out, and remains independent. However, it has lost exclusivity with the DAF DB250 chassis which is now marketed in Britain by Hughes

DAF, while the Delta body is now available on Mercedes chassis as the Prisma, and in modified form as the Sigma on Dennis Lance.

Quest 80

Quest 80 was another short-lived manufacturer, which flourished briefly in the 1980s. Primarily an exporter, it did build a few home market vehicles in the Telford factory which it occupied from 1979.

Much of its activity was in South Africa, so at that

Above:
One of the rather disastrous Quest 80 B-types built for Merseyside PTE. This one had returned to Merseyside and was operating on a Merseyside PTE service, though with David Tanner of St Helens, in October 1994.
S. J. Kelly

Below:
The prototype Quest 80 Model D, with Reeve Burgess bodywork, at the 1983 Brighton Coach Rally.

time when commercial activity with South Africa was frowned upon publicly little was heard of Quest 80. It developed a trolleybus chassis and the Q-Bus, which had a vertical Mercedes-derived Atlanta engine, side-mounted in the same style as the prewar AEC Q.

It was in 1983 that it entered the UK market with rear-engined bus and coach chassis, using Ford or Perkins engines. Prototypes were built with Locomotors and Reeve Burgess bodywork, and a Locomotors-bodied B-type was built for Ralphs Coaches for work at Heathrow Airport. This had a Ford 2726T six-litre engine and Allison gearbox.

The nearest thing Quest experienced to a break-through was when Excelsior of Bournemouth, a keen Ford user, wanted a more up-to-date Ford-powered chassis than Ford could provide. Excelsior managing director Vernon Maitland was a keen sailor and had found Ford diesels modified for marine use by Sabre to be effective power units, and so specified this 5.95litre 220bhp unit in his coaches, which were named after him, as type VM. They were rear-engined 12m air-sprung coaches with low driver positions, as was then fashionable, and 20 were sent for bodying for Excelsior by Plaxtons. Problems with them meant that two never entered service and a third was never bodied by Plaxtons.

Quest 80 tended to use Locomotors bodywork for bus chassis, and in 1984 Locomotors' parent UEI plc bought Quest 80, and three C-type Cummins-engined coach chassis were built at Locomotors' Andover factory before all production was transferred there that summer. A few D-type rear-engined buses, a straight-framed, leaf sprung chassis with vertical Ford 2723E or Perkins 6.354 engines and Ford synchro-mesh gearboxes were built for welfare customers, and the last vehicles completed were six B-types for Merseyside PTE with very square, oddly-proportioned Locomotors bodies. They had rear-mounted Perkins 6.354 engines, mounted on the nearside and driving through a U-drive arrangement which Quest 80 had developed to enable standard proprietary units to be used in a confined space. Again they were not a success, and Quest 80 production ended in 1985.

However, examples of another Quest type, the J-type, entered service after this. These were a shorter version of the D-type, also had Ford engines and the U-drive arrangement, and were bodied by Jonckheere, mostly with 37-seat bodies. They were heavily modified by Southampton coach operator Buddens, usually with a straight driveline using the Cummins B-series engine and 11 entered service in Britain and Ireland with independent coach operators up to 1988.

Quest 80 may have been an innovator, though something was obviously sadly lacking in its production. Of all the unusual British manufacturers this seems to have been the most disastrous, and a surprisingly large proportion of its output never reached completion.

Rowe

Another short-lived manufacturer was M. G. Rowe (Motors) Doublebois Ltd, which built a few Hillmaster bus and coach chassis in Cornwall in the 1950s. A prototype lightweight chassis was built in 1953, with a Meadows 4DC four-cylinder 5.7litre engine at the front and a five-speed Meadows

gearbox. It was bodied by Whitson with a full-front coach body, but before it was registered Rowe decided to develop underfloor-engined chassis. Thus the engine of the prototype was converted to horizontal format by Rowe itself, and went into the company's own fleet.

Meadows then produced its own horizontal version of the 4DC, the 4HDC, and the rest of Rowe's psv output was of mid-engined layout with entrances ahead of the front wheels. A Reading-bodied 44-seat bus was built for Millbrook Steamboat & Trading in 1956, followed by three for Morlais Motor Services, Merthyr Tydfil, in 1957/58. The operator built its own 44-seat bodies on Metal Sections frames. Production ended with these five, though lorry production was rather more significant, reaching three figures before the company went into receivership in 1960.

Rutland

The rear-engined Rutland Clipper was almost an exact contemporary of the first Rowe Hillmaster and was also bodied by Whitson. The 30ft coach chassis, built in Croydon by Motor Traction Ltd in 1954, had a vertical Perkins R6 108bhp engine driving through a David Brown four-speed synchromesh gearbox. In order to fit the driveline within the length of the rear overhang permitted on a 30ft chassis the drive was taken forward to a transfer box halfway along the chassis and then transmitted back into the front of the rear axle, a similar arrangement to that used on the Bristol RE in later years.

The 41-seat coach went to West Kent Motors of Biggin Hill and two more were built in 1954 and 1955, also bodied by Whitson.

SMT

Scottish Motor Traction built a 32-seat integral bus based on Albion components in 1955, though it was not announced officially until the following year. It had an aluminium alloy frame and used the same 65bhp four-cylinder horizontal diesel engine as the Albion Nimbus (also used in the horizontally-engined Claymore goods vehicle) and a four-speed synchromesh Albion gearbox. Perhaps the most interesting feature, apart from the very low unladen weight of 3tons 9¼cwt and fuel consumption around 22mpg, was the use of rubber suspension; independent suspension was considered but ruled out because of its complication and cost. It remained a one-off.

Left:
The first Rowe Hillmaster coach, still in service with its operator/builder in 1967.
M. A. Sutcliffe

Saunders-Roe

Saunders Roe was based in Beaumaris on Anglesey, and was best-known for its bus bodywork, particularly on Leyland Tiger Cub chassis, though it also built a sizeable number of RTs for London. However, in 1955 it built an integral bus, to a style identical to the Tiger Cub, for Maidstone & District. It had a Gardner 5HLW horizontal engine.

Seddon

The Oldham-based Seddon concern, which had moved from Salford just after the war, had built a small number of goods vehicles in the years leading up to the war. In 1946 a passenger chassis was developed, based largely on the 5-ton goods chassis, and fitted with a Perkins P6 engine and five-speed gearbox. It was a conventional, front-engined design, known as the Mark 4, and the first two were bodied by the company for a Scottish operator. It was suitable for 28-seat coach or 32-seat bus bodywork. A larger Mark 6 followed in 1950 when the maximum length limit was extended to 30ft. Quite a number were bodied by Seddon, which maintained a tradition of offering bodywork on its own chassis until virtually the end of production.

Although Bedford's Y-series chassis are sometime considered to have pioneered the use of vertical underfloor engines, Seddon was already building vehicles of that configuration by 1952, when it launched its Mark 10 and Mark 11 chassis. The Mark 10 had the Perkins P6 engine while the Mark 11 had the faster, 108bhp R6. The Mark 11 was intended for 30ft coachwork, the Mark 10 was about 3ft shorter, and both had the entrance ahead of the front axle, and quite a high chassis frame, with the engine protruding another 10in above it. The 1952 Show vehicle was a Mark 10 for West Riding, with Seddon's own 32-seat bodywork, though it was soon sold back to Seddon. Nevertheless the Mark 10 and Mark 11 remained in production until 1960, and about 100 were sold.

The Mark 19 was the next production underfloor-engined chassis, though only one, with an AEC horizontal engine, was built for the UK in 1959, and remains in service with its original operator, Thorne of Bubwith. It has an attractive Harrington body. All other Mark 19s were exported, and for much if its life as a bus producer Seddon was more active overseas than it was on the home market.

In 1958 Seddon bodied a batch of non-Seddon vehicles, six Albion Aberdonians for Manchester, and later renamed its bodybuilding organisation Pennine, to distance it from Seddon itself in order to build more on other manufacturers' chassis. The Pennine name was also applied to later chassis, and the Pennine 4 emerged in 1967. This was primarily a coach chassis in similar vein to the Ford R226, though available in lengths from 30ft to 36ft, with a Perkins 6.354 engine alongside the driver, ahead of the front axle, and driving originally through a five-speed constant-mesh gearbox, though later chassis had synchromesh. The 170bhp 8.5-litre Perkins V8.510 was also offered later, which gave it rather more performance than was usual from a lightweight chassis. An unusual customer for the type was SELNEC PTE, which adopted it as its standard coach chassis, some fitted with V8s, though one of the first operators was Gosport & Fareham which had some as service buses with Pennine bodies.

From the Pennine IV was developed what was reckoned to be the first midibus chassis. With no major mechanical components within the wheelbase it was quite a simple matter to produce a short version of it from 1972, which was sold as the Seddon Pennine 4.236, with a Perkins four-cylinder engine of that designation and either manual or Allison automatic gearbox. The most famous were the SELNEC Manchester Centreline vehicles, though others were sold to Edinburgh and Doncaster. All had Pennine bodies. By this time the full-sized Pennine had reached the Pennine VI, which was still front engined

Above:
An unusual Beadle-bodied, Perkins-engined Seddon Mk IV of Western National.
A. R. Packer

Left:
This Seddon Mk 10 appeared at the 1952 Commercial Motor Show. It had Seddon's own bodywork and carried West Riding livery. It is seen during the short period in which it actually worked for West Riding.
G. Holt

but available in lengths up to 12m. The engine was mounted very low in the frame to give a flat floor in the entrance area, though resulting in a very high floor level.

However, Seddon was not to remain just a light-weight producer; in 1969 it announced a rear-engined service bus, the Pennine RU. This was to be available in 33ft and 36ft form, with a horizontal Gardner 6HLX engine and five-speed Self-Changing Gears semi-automatic transmission. It was kept rather simpler than other rear-engined chassis of the 1960s, and had a straight chassis frame rather than one

Below:
Most Seddon Pennine RUs had Pennine bodywork, built by Seddon, though Lancashire United used this rather attractive Plaxton body instead. This one is seen operating on hire to SELNEC in Stockport on a former Stockport Corporation service.

Bottom:
Crosville was a major operator of RUs, this time with Pennine bodywork. EPG704 is a dual-purpose example, seen on the Rhyl-Ruthin service on 27 July 1971.
J. G. Carroll

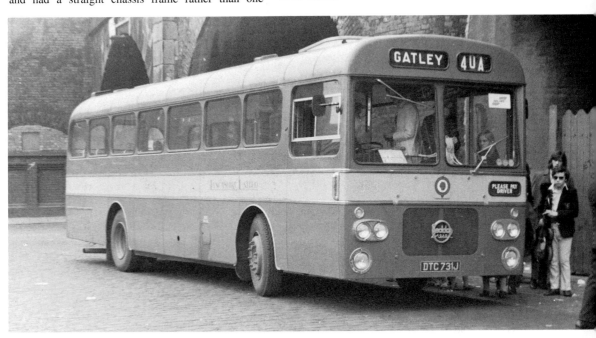

Top:
Also operated by Crosville, though built as a demonstrator, was this Seddon Pennine VII with underfloor Gardner engine and bodywork to RU style, though with a flat floor.
R. L. Wilson

Above:
The Seddon Pennine VII was more readily associated with Scottish Bus Group; this 1975-built vehicle for Eastern Scottish had one of the first Alexander T-type bodies.

Right:
Another Eastern Scottish Seddon
Pennine VII, this time with Plaxton
Supreme bodywork, in Taunton on
a tour to Torquay in 1978.
Ray Stenning

Below:
The midi version of the Seddon
Pennine IV, the 4.236, in service in
Manchester.
John Robinson

cranked over the rear axle; however, the chassis was inclined from front to rear so it still had the advantage of a low entrance, with a step-free interior too. The radiator was mounted on the side, and Seddon developed quite a stylish body for it. Darlington Transport was one satisfied customer, while other operators of it included Huddersfield and Doncaster Corporations, and most surprising, in view of its traditional Tilling loyalty to Bristol was Crosville which took 100 in bus and dual-purpose forms in 1971-72, when it was unable to obtain Bristol REs quickly enough. Another major customer was Lancashire United Transport, which took 50 with Plaxton bodywork. Production ended around 1974. Although Darlington was well-pleased with its RUs, and, as noted earlier, had the Ward Dalesman GRXI built as a replacement, others found it less reliable; all of Crosville's had to have their engines moved to permit a longer propshaft at a less sharp angle.

However, this wasn't to be Seddon's last heavyweight effort. Spurred on by the Scottish Bus Group, which required something resembling a Gardner-engined version of the Leyland Leopard, it built the Pennine VII, which had a mid-mounted Gardner 6HLXB engine and a choice of ZF four-speed or five speed synchromesh, favoured by SBG, or Self Changing Gears semi-automatic transmission. It was the first application of the horizontal version of the Gardner 6LXB, and the prototype appeared at the 1973 Scottish Motor Show with an Alexander Y-type dual-purpose body in Eastern Scottish livery, and most were built for the Scottish Bus Group with Alexander Y-type bodywork in bus or dual-purpose form or the later T-type. However, there were some full coach versions for SBG, including 12m vehicles with the impressive Alexander M-type motorway coach body for its London services and with Plaxton Supreme bodywork. SBG's requirement for a simple, straightforward vehicle meant that it had a mechanical handbrake, rather than the spring-type which was standard on most types by then, though spring brakes were available for less conservative operators. A few others were built for independent coach operators, again with Plaxton bodywork, while Crosville took an ex-demonstrator with a Pennine body, of very similar style to the body for the RU. Production ended in 1982. SBG had had some 500 Pennine VIIs. By now Seddon and Atkinson had merged and concentrated entirely on goods vehicles.

One small diversification worth mentioning was into electric vehicles. A battery-electric midibus based on a 4.236 was built in 1974, and a larger RU-based vehicle was built at the same time. Both were built for SELNEC PTE, the midibus putting in some useful service on the Centreline service, where its lack of range — despite holding records for battery vehicle range — was not a problem. The RU saw little service however.

Sentinel

It was only after the war that Shrewsbury-based Sentinel became known as a bus builder, and then only for a comparatively short period. It was better known before the war for its steam vehicles, both for road and rail, and although by the late 1930s steam power was very much outmoded for road transport Sentinel nonetheless built highly-sophisticated steam lorries. The relevance of these to our story is that Sentinel had developed horizontal steam engines that

Left:
Ribble's first Sentinel STC4 of 1949. This particular bus was bodied by Beadle, though subsequent ones were bodied by Sentinel to the same style.

Top:
The STC6 was rather more of a heavyweight; this one was built in 1951 for Boyer of Rothley, Leicestershire.

Above:
Sentinel also built a conventional coach chassis version of the STC6; this one was fitted with a Plaxton Venturer body for Warners of Tewkesbury in 1952.

could be tucked under the chassis of a lorry out of the way. Thus when it came to produce diesel engines Sentinel was able to adapt its steam engine technology and get ahead of the field to produce a workable underfloor-engined bus.

Sentinel caused something of a stir at the 1948 Commercial Motor Show at Earl's Court, by showing the first production underfloor-engined bus for the British market. Leyland was only able to show the horizontal engine for its forthcoming integral Olympic; Sentinel had got in ahead of Leyland, AEC and Bristol which were all developing underfloor-engined single-deckers. The Beadle-Sentinel at the 1948 show, for Western National, featured a four-cylinder, 6litre 90bhp indirect-injection engine with

five-speed overdrive gearbox and weighed in at only 5tons 8cwt, despite being a 40-seater. It had Sentinel's running units arranged in an integral structure by Beadle. Apart from a demonstrator and the first of a batch of six for Ribble, thereafter Sentinel built the bodywork itself, to Beadle's style, for service buses, though Beadle continued to body the SLC4 coach version. Ribble took its batch of six in 1949/50, though most STC4s were built for independent operators; the show exhibit was billed as 'one of

a fleet ordered for Western National', but remained a one-off.

When the dimensions regulations were relaxed to allow 30ft vehicles Sentinel moved on to a 30ft vehicle with a six-cylinder 9.12litre 135bhp indirect injection engine, the STC6 integral bus, with a four-speed constant-mesh gearbox. The coach version was a conventional chassis, the SLC6 with a five-speed overdrive gearbox, which with 135bhp on tap must have made for excellent performance. The same must have been true of the STC6, with a most impressive power to weight ratio, as it weighed only 5ton 15cwt. The STC4 and SLC4 remained in production, however. Ribble too was the most significant customer for the STC6, with 14 44-seat buses built in 1951, despite the fact that the Olympic was now available from Ribble's usual supplier, Leyland. The SLC6 was bodied conventionally by firms other than Beadle, and the SLC4 was also made available as a chassis; Adams of Barry took a Gurney Nutting-bodied SLC4 in 1951, while three SLC4s were bodied by Plaxtons with 37-seat centre-entrance bodies in 1952/53 and Bellhouse Hartwell bodied two SLC6s for Blue Cars, a London operator, in 1952/53.

From 1953, by which time 104 Sentinel psvs had been built, including 10 for export, all production was on separate chassis, the SLC6/30, which introduced a direct-injection version of the 9.12-litre six-cylinder engine, reducing the power output to 120bhp. Production was hardly rapid, however, and less than 30 were built for the home market before the company sold out to Rolls-Royce in 1956 and road-

vehicle construction finished. The majority were coaches with a variety of bodybuilders, including Plaxton, Duple and Whitson. Burlingham bodied nine of them as coaches, four of them for Schofield, Marsden. But four were bodied as buses, two unusually by Whitson, one by ACB, a dual-door demonstrator, and there was a particularly handsome one by Burlingham in 1955 which went to Green Bus, Rugeley, but ended its days with Yorkshire Traction.

Shelvoke & Drewry

Shelvoke & Drewry has always been a very specialist vehicle builder, particularly associated with refuse disposal, and came up with some highly innovative designs in the 1920s, some of which were built as buses mainly for seafront work.

It built only one bus postwar. In 1982 it was developing its SPV range for a whole host of highly-specialist applications, and this included a bus for airport transfer work. It had a front-mounted Ford engine and Allison automatic transmission. The chassis frame then cranked down behind the cab to give low access for passengers via a centre entrance. It had a full-width cab with no seating alongside the driver and received a Reeve Burgess body. It worked at Heathrow and Gatwick. It terrified the author when he drove it, so the less said about it the better.

Talbot

The rather complicated history of the Rootes Group ended up with a British offshoot of Peugeot called Talbot, which ceased building cars around 1985. One

Top left:
This splendid-looking 1952 SLC6 had stylish Bellhouse Hartwell bodywork for Blue Cars of London.

Left:
The Shelvoke & Drewry SPV airport bus with Reeve Burgess bodywork, built in 1981. It remained a one-off.

Below:
A TBP-built Talbot Express Pullman on an Essex County Council contracted service at Epping station.

Left:
A 1949 Tilling-Stevens K6LH7 with Dutfield bodywork. It was new to Kemps Motor Services, which was bought out of receivership in 1955 to become Chiltern Queens. It is seen, with a Leyland Comet behind, at Theale in 1960; it remained in service until 1964.
M. A. Sutcliffe

Below:
A 13-seat Trojan minibus at Outwood Mill, Surrey.
John Aldridge collection

product did remain however, the Italian-built Talbot Express, which was a van of Ford Transit dimensions which was also built as a Fiat and a Citroën. Unlike the Transit it was front-wheel drive, and as the front end was thus fully self-contained it was possible to get a proprietary-built aluminium-framed chassis extension with two pairs of wheels. This made the basis of a very useful minibus; with no driveline to get in the way a truly low-floor minibus could be produced, with no interior steps. The Talbot Express Pullman resulted in 1986.

Although used largely as a welfare vehicle it has excellent psv applications too, and was bought by a number of operators, not least Barrow Borough Transport, Kentish Bus and BET's short-lived Zippy operation in Preston. It is also often used on County Council tenders requiring a low-floor vehicle; the Talbot is a much cheaper alternative to much more expensive low-floor buses and just as effective where high capacity is not required.

Production was too small for a volume manufacturer, so in 1990 it was taken over by TBP of West Bromwich, which announced a successor based on the new Peugeot Boxer which finally replaced the Talbot in 1994.

Thornycroft

Most of Basingstoke-based Thornycroft's output of buses was prewar, though it also built a few of its Nippy HF lorry chassis for psv use, with small bodies with up to about 20 seats, between 1946 and 1950. MacBraynes was a user, which also took a specific psv chassis which Thornycroft introduced in the late 1940s. The Nippy had a four-cylinder 3.9litre petrol engine and four-speed gearbox.

Thornycroft built two new double-deck chassis in 1947, with its own 7.8litre diesel engine, fluid flywheel and an unconventional design of gearbox. Five similar single-deck chassis were built; bodied as coaches they operated for some years for the Bristol Co-Operative Society. Thornycroft was taken over by AEC in 1961.

Tilling-Stevens

Tilling-Stevens of Maidstone is another manufacturer which was best-known for its prewar products and is especially associated with the early days of motorbuses for its unusual petrol-electric concept. By the time World War 2 broke out it was a spent force, although it built a small number of coaches after the war. Unlike those pioneering efforts its postwar vehicles were entirely conventional, even conservative, in their approach, and despite Tilling-Stevens' involvement in the development of what became the Commer TS3 horizontal engine, they all had conventional vertical front engines.

Its first postwar models were the K5LA7 and K6LA7, which were introduced in September 1947. The K5LA7 was intended primarily as a half-cab single-deck service bus, though some were fitted with coach bodywork, and this had a Gardner 5LW five-cylinder 7.0litre engine and five-speed David Brown constant-mesh gearbox. The K6LA7 was a coach version with the larger six-cylinder, 8.4litre Gardner 6LW. The next year it made a version available with a larger Meadows 6DC.630 130bhp 10.35litre direct-injection diesel, the K6MA7. It appeared at the 1948 Commercial Motor Show with a Dutfield body featuring a radio and fluorescent lighting.

The various K-series models sold only to independent operators; no orders were forthcoming from the major operators, and in 1950 Tilling-Stevens had a go at the lightweight market with the Express Mark II. This was a full-fronted front-engined 30ft-long chassis, aimed at a similar market to the Bedford SB, introduced at the same time, and had a small four-cylinder Meadows 4D.330 5.4litre 80bhp diesel engine and five-speed constant-mesh gearbox. Despite a very low selling price and simple specification it too was destined not to sell very well and in 1953 Tilling-Stevens sold out to the Rootes Group. Its factory was turned over to production of the Commer TS3 engine.

Trojan

Trojan of Croydon was well-known as a lightweight van manufacturer in the 1950s. The bonneted one-ton model and the $1^1/4$ton forward control model were offered as 13-seat psvs, and often marketed as a complete vehicle. All were unusually fitted with the two-stroke three-cylinder Perkins P3 engine. The forward-control chassis was also said to be bodied by Trojan itself; two all-Trojan coaches were at Earls Court in 1960, one for Scotts Greys of Darlington, the other for Edinburgh Corporation.

Volvo

During the 1980s there was much argument as to whether Volvo should be counted as a British manufacturer or not; it sourced some of its components in Britain and although based in Sweden built lorries in large numbers at its Scottish plant (see 'Ailsa').

For our purposes we will examine only those Volvo models built in Britain, which excludes Volvo's first model offered in Britain, the highly-regarded B58 mid-engined coach chassis. As noted earlier on there was a close tie-up between Volvo and Ailsa, which was a British marque, in those early days and now the former Ailsa factory is once again used by Volvo for psv production in Britain.

Volvo replaced the B58 with the yet more successful B10M in 1980. This again was a Swedish chassis, though B10M parts were assembled into British-built Citybus double-deckers for a time.

However, Volvo was to become very much more significant in the history of the British bus. Leyland Bus had been sold to its management on 13 January 1987, a very difficult time in the British bus market. In 1988 Volvo made a very generous offer to buy Leyland from its management, so on 30 March 1988 Leyland Bus was sold to Volvo. Volvo had great intentions for Leyland, and as part of its strategy for the company began production of the B10M at Workington in 1990. The idea was that all UK market production would take place there, as well as some for certain other markets. VL Bus & Coach took over Leyland's sales from 1 January 1989, but on 1 July 1991 the Volvo Bus Ltd name replaced it; however, the Leyland name remained on Leyland's remaining models. But in a shock announcement on 6 December 1991 it became known that Leyland's last manufacturing plant, Workington, was to close, spelling the end of the Tiger and Lynx.

The Lynx was replaced in the UK market by the Swedish-built Volvo B10B chassis, and B10M production was once again concentrated on Sweden. However, this was not the end of the story for Volvo production in Britain. The Leyland Olympian was to continue, albeit revamped as a Volvo, and 60% of its components were sourced from Volvo. The Gardner engine option was dropped in favour of Volvo's own TD102KF 9.6-litre engine, alongside the Cummins L10 which remained available. Production was moved to Irvine, which became partly a bus factory again, and the first Olympian was driven off the production line there on 22 March 1993.

Volvo had announced a new rear-engined midibus in 1992. When it had acquired Leyland Volvo was keen to use some of the engineering expertise there, and there was some Leyland influence in both the design of this and also the new full-size B10B. Volvo's new Volvo B10L low-floor bus also owes some of its design to Leyland. The new midibus was a direct challenger to the Dennis Dart, though featured air suspension and the option of ZF automatic transmission as well as Allison. Unlike the Dart it could be built as a full 2.5m wide vehicle, and was also available with manual transmission as a small coach. It was to be built in Austria as the B6R, though after a few pre-production buses were built there all production moved to Irvine, and the name was changed to B6. Production began simultaneously with the Olympian and soon built up to substantial volumes. The B6 has much in common with the bigger B10M, though the engine is a vertical six-litre TD63E mounted in-line at the rear with options of 180bhp or 210bhp.

However, B10M production restarted at Irvine in 1995; the first was due out in August, and a low-floor version of the B6, the B6LE, also appeared in 1995. Volvo is the biggest supplier now to the British market and is second only to Dennis for bus production in the UK; 20 years ago one would not have thought of either of them as significant in the British bus market!

Right:
A Volvo B6 in service with Cambus. The Cambus B6s were the first to have the Marshall body derived from the original Duple design for the Dennis Dart.

Centre right:
An all-Scottish product of Henderson Travel, Lanark; a Volvo B6 with Alexander Dash bodywork.

Below:
For a time the Volvo B10M was built at Workington. Some of those built in Britain formed the basis of National Expressliners; this one was used on Caledonian Express services by Tayside Travel Services. The concept of the Expressliner was a standard National Express coach with Plaxton bodywork leased to operators on the National Express network through Plaxton's Roadlease subsidiary.
S. L. Render

Above:
A Northern Counties Palatine II-bodied Volvo Olympian for Bristol CityLine, used on Park-&-Ride work.

Below:
Alexander's 'de luxe' version of the R-type, the Royale, was originally built for Yorkshire Coastliner on Volvo Olympians. The first is seen here entering service at Leeds in 1993.